Meet the Goldfish

Goldfish are the most common household pet in the world.

There are hundreds of varieties of goldfish to choose from.

All of the goldfish varieties, it is thought, have been generated from a single species—the Crucian Carp, a fish that originated in Asia thousands of years ago.

Goldfish, known also as the *Carassius auratus,* still can be found in streams and ponds throughout Asia.

The Chinese were the first to domesticate goldfish. The fish were usually kept in ponds or pools in courtyards.

Goldfish didn't find their way to Europe until the eighteenth century, and it wasn't until 1878 that goldfish were imported to America.

Goldfish are a fairly hardy species and are quite adaptable to different temperatures, water and food.

Even though they are all simply goldfish, the different varieties have unique swimming abilities, modified body composition and distinct temperaments.

Goldfish should be housed with goldfish, not with tropical fish—it is even important to keep the same types of goldfish in groups together.

You don't have to spend hours grooming or housebreaking a goldfish—maintaining its aquarium is a snap.

Consulting Editor
MADDY HARGROVE

Featuring Photographs by
AARON NORMAN

Howell Book House
An Imprint of Macmillan General Reference USA
A Pearson Education Macmillan Company
1633 Broadway
New York, NY 10019-6785

Library of Congress Cataloging-in-Publication Data
The essential goldfish / featuring photographs by Aaron Norman.
    p. cm.
  ISBN 1-58245-083-8
  1. Goldfish. 2. Aquariums.
  I. Norman, Aaron. 1929-
  II. Howell Book House
SF458.G6E77 1999   99-11011
639.3'7484—dc21   CIP

Manufactured in the United States of America
10 9 8 7 6 5 4 3 2 1

Series Director: Michele Matrisciani
Production Team: Tammy Ahrens, Carrie Allen, and
    Heather Pope
Book Design: Paul Costello
Illustration: Jeff Yesh

ARE YOU READY?!

- ☐ Have you prepared your home and your family for your new pet?

- ☐ Have you gotten the proper supplies you'll need to care for your fish?

- ☐ Have you learned about setting up and maintaining your fish's aquarium?

- ☐ Have you thought about the ways in which you can protect your fish from disease?

- ☐ Have you arranged a schedule to accommodate your new fish-keeping hobby?

No matter what stage you're at with your fish—still thinking about getting one, or it's already part of the family—this Essential guide will provide you with the practical information you need to understand and care for your pet. Of course you're ready—you have this book!

THE ESSENTIAL

Goldfish

The Goldfish's Senses

SIGHT

The eyes of fish operate somewhat like humans' except that they lack eyelids and their irises work much slower than our own. Fish are near-sighted, but can detect color. Since their eyes are on either side of their heads, they have monocular vision as opposed to binocular vision like humans.

SOUND

Hearing is an essential tool for goldfish survival. Goldfish have no outward ears. Their hearing lies entirely inside the skull. Sound vibrations pass through the water, through the fish's body and reverberate in this inner ear.

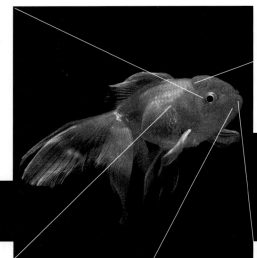

TOUCH

Goldfish possess a lateral line, which is a series of dimples in somewhat of a line across the fish's side. These dimples are thermosensory nerve endings connected to the brain, and when pressure is exerted on them, or when vibrations occur, the fish can feel them right away.

TASTE

Most of a goldfish's tastebuds are located on the lips and all over the mouth; they don't have tongues. There are even tastebuds on the outsides of the lips, which is an advantage for the goldfish in the hunt for food and for a mate.

SMELL

A goldfish has nostrils called nares. But unlike humans, who breathe through their noses, goldfish cannot. The sense of smell is strong with goldfish, and is highly important in the search for food and in mating.

CHAPTER ONE

Getting to Know the Goldfish

Goldfish are the most common household pet in the world, and there are hundreds of beautiful varieties. The keeping of goldfish is the most popular form of pet ownership in the world. The size of the aquarium can vary, depending on the size of the room, and can be kept with relatively little maintenance. Goldfish don't need to be housebroken, they won't beg at the table and you'll never have to cover up the sofa when you aren't home.

The great thing about goldfish is that they are a very hardy species, and are quite adaptable to many different water conditions. They are excellent candidates for outdoor ponds or pools, in almost any seasonal climate. Given the wide range of colors, body shapes and general disposition, there is in fact a goldfish for everyone.

THE HISTORY OF AQUARIUM KEEPING

It is believed that the ancient Egyptians were the first people to keep aquarium fish in captivity. Many Egyptians kept goldfish and other types of species in small ponds to help achieve better social status among their neighbors and close friends.

The fishkeeping craze really began to spread a short time later when the Orientals became fascinated with the common goldfish. These ingenious people began breeding new varieties of goldfish at a very rapid rate. In a short period of time, the common-looking goldfish was a thing of the past. Newer, fancier varieties began to appear and captivated the hearts of people worldwide.

During the late 1880s, public aquariums began to open in several European countries. There were very few aquatic species available for display during that time period, but these institutions still attracted amazingly large crowds. People began to take an interest in keeping fish and frantically searched for ways to maintain them in their homes.

Private aquarium keeping quickly spread, and the first dedicated tropical fish hobbyists began to make their appearance.

The first home aquariums were quite different from the ones we have today. During the early part of the century, tanks were poorly constructed and were often heated with open flames. This poor safety practice often led to the destruction of many homes. Early aquarium keepers had no filters, internal heaters, hoods, lighting or medications that they could rely on, so captive species did not live for long periods of time.

Aquarium conditions finally began to improve during the early 1900s when tropical fish shows began to appear on a regular basis. During these social events, enthusiasts were able to get together with other fishkeepers and share their knowledge and aquarium keeping skills. A short while later, these early fishkeepers formed aquarium societies, which helped to demand better standards from manufacturers of aquarium equipment and supplies. With the high-tech equipment and well-made tanks that are available today, hobbyists are able to maintain home aquariums with relative ease.

THE CLASSIFICATION OF THE GOLDFISH

Goldfish, known also as the *Carassius auratus,* still can be found in streams and ponds throughout their region of origin, Asia. In the wild, their colors are somewhat duller. The goldfish comes from the Cyprinidae family, a classification of carp. They are descended from the Crucian Carp, also known as *Carassius carassius,* and are related to the Common Carp, which is known as *Cyprinus carpio,* and to the minnow.

The best way to distinguish between a carp and a goldfish is to look at the dorsal fin. The goldfish's dorsal is usually straight up or is concave (curved in) while the carp's dorsal is generally convex (curved out).

THE GOLDFISH'S BODY AND ITS STRUCTURE

The different varieties of goldfish, which are all unique, fall outside the general physiognomy of fish altogether. We will use the Comet Goldfish as the classic example of a goldfish when we discuss them in general terms. Comets are the common American variety.

3

Comet Goldfish, like the one shown here, are considered the most common American variety of goldfish.

These Shubunkin Goldfish are one of many varieties of exotic goldfish species.

4

The Comet's body is stream-lined, being more or less flat on the sides. The view from the top shows the middle as somewhat thicker than the head or tail section. The view from the side shows the middle as somewhat deeper, whereas the body tapers toward the head and the section where the body meets the tail. This narrow section is also known as the caudal peduncle.

Regardless of variety, especially among the fancies, the caudal peduncle is almost always narrow, no matter how large the body. Some Fantails, especially the Redcap and the Marigold Chinese Lionhead, have exceptionally large heads, while Fantail, Moor and Veiltail, which are quite round, vary in their head shapes and sizes.

Fins

Fins have three main functions: sta-bilization, braking and propulsion. They come in two types, paired and median, and they are located at five places on the fish's body.

The pectoral fins are those found closest to the gills and are an excel-lent example of paired fins. They are almost always moving, because they help the fish to turn, hover, navigate tight corners or propel backward. While they can help in forward propulsion, it is not their main function. The pectorals are also used for fanning eggs and dislodging food from the bottom of the tank. The pectorals are usually found somewhere underneath or just behind and below the gills, on each side, toward the bottom of the body. They are not always shaped the same on different varieties. They can be short and small as on a Lionhead, or long and flowing as on a Veiltail.

The dorsal fin is an excellent example of the median fin. It rises directly from the top of the middle of the fish's back. It is made up of rigid and soft spines webbed with membrane. When a goldfish is healthy, this fin stands straight up, and its main function is to help stabilize the fish. It keeps the fish from rolling over by keeping the bottom of the fish down. Whether hovering or during forward propulsion, it keeps the fish moving straight.

The pelvic fins are a pair of fins located near the abdomen, toward the bottom of the fish, generally in front of the anal canal. More than

anything they act as brakes, but they also stabilize and help in turning. While ventral or pelvic fins may be elongated, as on a Veiltail Ryukin, they rarely grow so large that they impair or grow beyond use, as opposed to the dorsal and caudal fins. Pelvic fins in other species of tropical fish are used for carrying eggs and threatening predators and rivals.

The anal fin protrudes from the bottom of the body in front of the anal and sexual openings. It is a median fin, and its main job is to function as a stabilizer. On some varieties, these fins can aid in propulsion and turning in small spaces. Sometimes, in the fancy varieties, the anal fin becomes a set of paired fins. Interestingly, they grow from the spot where there would

Some varieties of goldfish, like this Celestial, have no dorsal fin, and consequently have more difficulty swimming.

This Shubunkin uses its pectoral fins to turn itself and navigate while swimming in its tank.

have been a median fin, and are the only set of paired fins that are actually joined together where they meet the body. Sometimes the fins themselves are actually joined along the backside of the fin for a short distance, but never for the length of it.

The caudal or tail fin is actually a median fin. The caudal or tail fin is extremely important in propulsion, and is usually the source for most of the power during swimming. It can also act as a brake, but is much more helpful in turning. While fancy varieties might have a fantail or some other elongated tail, like the anal fin, it is really a median

fin. The fins can sometimes be forked, as in the Black Moor, or can be wide and fan-shaped, as in the Veiltail. In the fancier varieties, these fins are so exaggerated that they are not as helpful, if at all, and consequently, these fish are slow swimmers and would not survive in the wild.

There are three different types of caudal fins: the single tail fin, the veiltail and the fantail. There are varieties of each of these, but these are the three main types. The single tail fin is obvious, and can be found on the Common Goldfish. The fantail is the most common of the fancy varieties. This is a pair of forked tails joined at the caudal peduncle. The veiltail is a beautiful, large tail, which has no indentations (or forks) and is square finished. It is usually very long and elegant.

Scales

The body of a goldfish is covered with overlapping scales. The scales are composed of a hard, bony substance. They serve to protect the fish, reducing the chance of injuries or infection.

These are covered by epidermal tissue. Numerous glands secrete mucus and produce the slimy effect we view as slippery. The slimy coating helps the fish to swim more easily in the water, reducing the friction between its body and the water itself. The slimy coating also acts to guard against injury or infection.

The scale is actually transparent; the color of the goldfish usually comes from the dermis, the lower or inner layer of skin. The forward end of each scale is attached to the dermis. The scales overlap each other like shingles on a house, providing a solid wall of protection as well as comfortable movement. "The wild form of the goldfish," according to Neil Teitler, a goldfish expert, "has

The Black Moor exhibits an abundance of melanophores, a type of skin pigment. Notice this fish's long, large, forked caudal fin.

between 28 and 31 scales along the lateral line and 6 scales between the dorsal spine and the lateral line." Fear, excitement and high hormone activity can cause your goldfish to temporarily change color. The lateral line is a series of indentations having to do with the senses and will be discussed later.

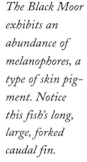

7

This white morph Comet exhibits a shiny, scaly exterior—characteristics of a metallic fish.

SLEEPING

If there is quiet time in your house, usually at night, you may find your fish at the bottom of the tank, among some rocks or plants. Since they have no eyelids, many people think the fish are always awake. Fish do not sleep per say, but are actually in a state of suspended animation which provides them with rest. A short recovery time is needed to revive from this state, which leaves them vulnerable to predators. Goldfish tend to lose some color and luster when resting at night. Occasionally the pectoral or tail fins will move to keep the fish balanced.

To grow to their potential and have the best color they can develop, it is important that your goldfish have room to exercise and rest. Goldfish need their rest, just like you, so turn the light off during the evening hours and let your fish relax. If you don't turn the light off, the fish will rest for shorter periods of time or largely go without, which could result in shorter life spans, less color and less active fish. If you are trying to breed your fish, suitable resting periods are of the utmost importance.

For every variety of goldfish, the specific number of scales remains the same within that group, from fish to fish. For each season of growth in a goldfish (approximately one year, provided that there is a six- to eight-week drop in temperature), the goldfish develops a ring in its scales. The number of rings on the scale determines the age of the fish. These rings are called circuli.

SCALE TYPES—Goldfish can be characterized based on four different kinds of scale groups: metallic, matt, nacreous and calico.

Metallic fish exhibit a shiny, scaly exterior, such as is seen in the Comet. These scales contain a crystalline substance called guanine. Guanine is responsible for the sheen of the scales. The more guanine, the shinier the scale.

Some scales lack guanine almost entirely. They are called matt scales and exhibit no reflective tissue anywhere on the fish's body; rather, they have a flat or skinlike look to them. They lack intensive coloration and do not seem as hardy as other fish. Matt fish are sometimes referred to as scaleless even though they are not.

When metallic- and matt-type scales are both found on a goldfish, it is known as nacreous. Some individual scales, or whole sections of

All the fins contribute to the goldfish's swimming and maneuvering through water. This Lionhead Oranda has beautiful, fine fins.

the body, might feature a metallic-type finish, while others might feature a matt-type finish.

Swim Bladder

A swim bladder is a gas-filled sac that helps a goldfish rise or fall in its watery environment. In a goldfish, there are actually two swim bladders, one directly in front of the other. These compartments contain oxygen, carbon dioxide and nitrogen.

By inflating the swim bladder, the goldfish rises; when the goldfish deflates the swim bladder, descent is made easier. This also helps the fish stabilize and hover comfortably. Some elaborate varieties are top-heavy, and as a result, will always swim at an angle. An example of this is the Lionhead, which has a smaller forward sac, causing its head to thrust slightly at a downward angle. The swim bladder is also known to aid in the hearing process by amplifying sound in many species.

FIVE GOOD REASONS TO KEEP GOLDFISH

They are easy to care for

Goldfish do not require a lot of space

Fishkeeping is educational

Goldfish do not make noise

Fishkeeping is a challenge

OTHER ORGANS—Although goldfish are different from tropical fishes in terms of anatomy, they possess circulatory, respiratory, digestive and nervous systems common to most members of this vertebrate group.

HOW DO GOLDFISH SWIM?

The back-and-forth movement of the tail fin provides the goldfish with forward motion. The fish literally pulls the tail from one side of its body to the other. By going back and forth, the tail pushes the water behind it, thus pushing the fish forward. By bending the tail appropriately, the fish also steers itself.

The dorsal fin keeps the fish right-side up, and the pectoral, ventral and anal fins help to thrust and steer, as well as stop. The pectoral fins are used for tight turning and hovering.

The fish stops by reversing the tail motion, quickly. All other fins immediately become rigid. Sometimes the pectoral fins are instrumental in backing up and are at times used when a quick or sudden stop is needed, much like a thruster rocket on a spaceship.

HOW DO GOLDFISH BREATHE?

Goldfish, like all fish, require oxygen to live. Since they live in the water, they do not breathe as we do. Instead of lungs, they have gills. These organs extract oxygen from the water and expel carbon dioxide from their own system, much like other aquatic vertebrates. As the fish swims, it opens its mouth, taking in vast amounts of water. An oral membrane automatically closes off the water from going down the proverbial wrong pipe.

The water passes through the gills, which in the goldfish are located on either side of the head. The gills are filled with tiny membranes.

As the water passes over these membranes and filaments, oxygen is exchanged for carbon dioxide. As the blood passes through the filaments, they oxygenate the blood while releasing all the other unwanted gases. A minute amount of breathing takes place through the skin.

When there is insufficient oxygen in the water, fish rise to just below the surface, their mouths actually protruding from the water, gulping for air. These fish are actually trying to avoid suffocation. This circumstance most often occurs in the well-known "goldfish bowl." We will talk about the dangers and problems of the goldfish bowl in another chapter.

COLOR

The coloration of a goldfish, or any fish for that matter, depends on a wide variety of circumstances. Water composition and temperature greatly affect a fish's chromatophores (pigment cells), as do diet and environment.

The Calico category has gained in popularity, and its classification contains any goldfish with three or more colors appearing anywhere on the body.

CHAPTER TWO

The Varieties of Goldfish

There are no official divisions among varieties of goldfish, but there are several different groupings of goldfish one should understand before beginning.

It is important to group these fish together in the same way you would set up an aquarium for a beginner, or, for that matter, an experienced fish enthusiast or an

A Fantail (left) is a better swimmer than a Lionhead (right), and would be more likely to get the "lion's share" of the food.

expert. In fact, these are the groups that have been suggested by pet store owners nationwide and acknowledged by goldfish enthusiasts.

For example, the Comet, the Common Goldfish and the Shubunkin (both Bristol and London types) are all in the same category. These are strong, hardy swimmers, competitive fish, and should definitely not be kept with a Lionhead or Veiltail, as these are slower swimmers and will not be able to compete for food at the same level. Consult your local pet store owner before pairing unlike fish.

The following is a small sampling of the many different types of goldfish available, but many of the most commercially available are included, as well those that are actually quite rare.

BODY TYPE AND FINNAGE

There are four basic goldfish body types. The first is the *flat* body type, including the Common Goldfish, the Comet and the Shubunkin. The second is the *round* or *egg-shaped* body type, like the Oranda and the Veiltail. The third is shaped like the egg-shaped group but lacks a dorsal fin, like the Lionhead and the Celestial. The fourth is the obtruding eye group, which includes the Bubble Eye and Telescope Eye. The distinction here is very important. Goldfish that lack a dorsal fin do not swim as well as their cousins with dorsal fins. This is always a very important consideration that should be taken when setting up goldfish.

13

Single-Tail, Flat-Bodied Goldfish

These types of goldfish are among the hardiest of all goldfish families. They are the fastest swimmers and are the most streamlined. As a result they are very competitive and successful in the hunt for food as compared with more exotic species. They all tend to be extremely easy to care for, and are excellent choices for beginners. These are also the breeds that tend to be better for ponds and the group that tends to grow the largest.

The Common Goldfish is the hardiest of all goldfish. Its life expectancy is somewhere between five and ten years if properly maintained. It can withstand temperatures as low as 40°F and as high as 80°F. These are ideal candidates for outdoor ponds, as they are able to withstand great temperature changes.

Long, sleek and flat-bodied, the Common Goldfish is the closest cousin in the goldfish family to the carp. When young, they tend to be a bluish color. As they age, goldfish will turn to a metallic orange. It is often sold as a feeder for other carnivorous fish.

The Common Goldfish is tapered at the head and caudal

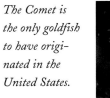

The Comet is the only goldfish to have originated in the United States.

A Shubunkin Goldfish. The name Shubunkin *is Japanese, and means deep red with different colors.*

peduncle, is flat-bodied and is wider in the middle. It is deeper in height and wider in width than the Comet. Its fins are classic: an erect dorsal fin, a single forked tail, well-proportioned pectoral and ventral fins. They are not overly large fins, but rather just what is necessary. These goldfish are fast swimmers and very competitive. In a pond they can grow as large as 12 to 14 inches, and in a large aquarium, 6 to 9 inches, depending on the size of the tank.

The Comet is the only goldfish to have originated in the United States. It was developed in the 1880s by the U.S. Fisheries Department. At about the same time, Hugo Mulrett, an American breeder, developed what happened to be the same type of strain. It is Mr. Mulrett who gave the Comet its name. In Japan it is called *tetsugyo*. Comets were placed in the reflecting pond on the Mall in Washington, D.C.

The Comet looks very much like a Common Goldfish, except that it is generally longer and sleeker, and has more exaggerated fins. The fins are approximately twice as long as those of a Common Goldfish, but the fin types are the same. The tail fin is especially large and beautiful, sometimes as large or larger than the body. It has the same metallic orange color as well. Comets come in silver (white) and yellow, as well as in combinations of these colors. While they are usually metallic, nacreous Comets are not at all uncommon.

Like the Common Goldfish, the Comet is a fast swimmer and is very hardy, able to withstand great changes in temperature, from as low as 50°F to as high as 80°F. Comets are excellent pond or aquarium fish. The Comet is somewhat smaller than the Common Goldfish, and in a pond will only grow to about 7 to 10 inches in length.

There are two types of Shubunkins, the London and the Bristol.

Originally thought to be bred in Japan around the turn of the century, these fish became very popular in England.

Basically the Shubunkin is a common Western goldfish that is calico or nacreous. They are long, sleek and flat-sided. Their most attractive feature is the variety of hues in which they appear. The colors are mostly deep reds, yellows, whites, and dark blues, violets or blacks. It is often said that the more dark hues a Shubunkin has (violets, blues or blacks), the more valuable it is in the marketplace. In some circles, this fish is also known as the Harlequin.

The difference between the Bristol and the London type of Shubunkin is that the Bristol's tail fin is much larger than the London's tail. The Bristol's is a forked, wide tail, but not very long, while the more popular London variety has a smaller, more squared-off tail.

Shubunkins tend to grow to a maximum size of 6 inches long, and are excellent swimmers. They are very strong and require room to swim. With proper care, the Shubunkin is one of the most long-lived of all domestic fish, living sometimes between ten and twenty years. They are ideal for outdoor pools and ponds and are hardy enough to suffer great temperature changes within a year's cycle.

The Wakin is the common goldfish of Japan, and Wakin is its

16

The Fantail is among the most popular fancy breed available to the hobbyist.

Japanese name. This variety was first developed in China, so the name is very tongue-in-cheek. Bluish in color when very young, it will grow to a deep vermillion red. Some strains of this variety have white patches. In all respects it is very much like the common Western goldfish that we know, except that it has a double caudal or tail fin. Despite their double tail, the Wakin swim fast enough to be kept with single-tail, flat-bodied fish.

The Jikin is known more commonly as the Butterfly Tail Goldfish. It is also known as the Peacock-Tailed Goldfish. It is very similar to the Wakin in all respects, and is thought to be bred from the Wakin. The easily understood difference is the tail. When fully opened, it forms a large X, and looks very much like a butterfly. These are hardy fish and are good starter fish, but are not as easily found as Common or Comets.

There is little difference between this breed and the Comet, except for coloration. The Tancho has a bright red cap, and its body is usually silver or white. Pink can sometimes be found on the body or on the fins. The forked tail of a Tancho is also smaller than the Comet's.

FIVE WAYS TO ENHANCE YOUR FISHKEEPING HOBBY

Scuba diving and snorkeling

Join an aquarium club

Visit a public aquarium

Take photos of your fish

Try breeding a new species

The name *Tancho* comes from the Japanese crane, which has a red spot on its head. Many breeds have a Tancho coloration, including koi.

17

Round or Egg-Shaped Body Type

DORSAL-FINNED GOLDFISH

The next two groups hold some of the more exotic varieties in the entire fish lexicon, tropical fish included. They include a numbing variety of tails, body shapes, eye shapes, head shapes, etc. You can see how one's fascination with goldfish alone can easily last a lifetime.

The round or egg-shaped varieties look just like what is suggested here: They look like an egg with fins. They have short, rounded bodies,

A hump back and wide tail are classic traits of the Ryukin.

and it is difficult to distinguish head from body in some varieties.

This group tends to represent the moderate swimmers. They are faster than some more exotic varieties, but not as fast as their more streamlined cousins. What this group lacks in streamlined form, it makes up for in exaggerated finnage and bright bold colorings.

The other thing to remember is that this group, save the Fantail and the Black Moor (depending on where you live), is really not suitable for most outdoor ponds or pools.

They tend to need slightly warmer water, and some are not as hardy as the previous group's fishes.

Dating back some 1,300 to 1,500 years, the Fantail is one of the oldest goldfish varieties known to man. The Fantail is called *loochoo* in Chinese, and its metallic orange color should grow very deep and bright.

Shaped like an egg, this fish has a large, double caudal or tail fin. The tail should be long and flowing. Fantails are one of the more popular goldfish on the market. The body is

the most streamlined of the entire
final two groupings, and is still more
roundish in shape.

In the best specimens of the
breed the fish's tail should not be
joined at any juncture along either
side, but rather only at the caudal
peduncle. The anal fins should be
paired as well and, again, not joined
in any place, but should be matching
and on separate sides.

The most popular Fantails are
the solid orange metallic. They are
the most plentiful and the hardiest.
The Fantail is also available in
nacreous; again, those showing the
most blues and blacks are considered
to be among the most prized.
Nacreous Fantails are not as hardy
as their orange metallic relations.

This is the only one of the fancy
breeds that is durable and hardy
enough for outdoor ponds. It is also
the first fancy variety any hobbyist
should own before moving into the
more exotic breeds. With good care,
a Fantail will grow to 3 to 6 inches
in length, and has a life expectancy
of somewhere between five and ten
years.

It is thought that the Nymphs
were a cross between a Comet and a
Fantail. The Nymph has a short
body, is roundish with a deep belly

and a short head and has a large
mouth with full lips and erect nostrils. It has extremely long fins, and
a dorsal fin that sits far back on the
spine. Its pectoral and ventral fins
are long, as is its single anal fin. The
Nymph comes in single-tail, fantail
and fringe-tailed varieties.

The Ryukin is the Japanese version of the Fantail. Some argue that
it is the older version of the Fantail.
Legend has it that they were first
developed on the Ryuku Islands,
hence the name. The main difference is that this variety has a high,
arching back, from which the dorsal
fin extends even higher.

The back appears almost like a
hump, which begins just after the
head. Also, the tail is wider, mean-
ing that it becomes longer vertically
instead of horizontally. Because of
the body shape, the fins sometimes
appear more toward a right angle
than the average Fantail. The body
is very heavy in this species.

The Ryukin can grow to
between 3 and 6 inches long and
will live five to ten years or longer.
Ryukins are available in all the same
color variations as the average
Fantail, including Tancho, and are
very popular. Ryukins are also
excellent beginner fish for anyone

wanting to move toward keeping the more exotic breeds. They are also good for outdoor ponds or pools.

The origin of the Veiltail is somewhat under debate. Some claim, like Anmarie Barrie and John Coborn, both goldfish experts, that the Veiltail is actually a mutation of the Fantail, while Marshall Ostow, another goldfish authority, claims that the Veiltail was bred from the Wakin, the Japanese common goldfish. Regardless, the Veiltail looks more like a Fantail to the novice and for description's sake.

The most striking feature of the Veiltail is the finnage. The dorsal fin extends very high, usually straight up on a good specimen. All the other fins—the pectoral, the paired anal and the caudal—are long and extend in beautiful flowing ribbons downward. It has a double caudal fin and its paired anal fins extend so far back that they are even with the middle of the elongated tail. There are no forks in the tail.

Easily considered one of the most beautiful of all goldfish, these are not the hardiest of fish. They are not the most delicate, but they do need more care than the average goldfish. They require space to swim because of their long finnage, so the aquarium should not be overcrowded with other fish or too many plants. The quality of the water must be maintained, so that they don't lose their color. Their fins are very susceptible to rot and any number of fungal diseases.

The colorations of Veiltails range from orange and red metallic to black to nacreous. The rounder the body, the more ball-shaped, the better that specimen is thought to be.

They will live somewhere between four and six years and will grow to somewhere between 3 and 5 inches long, not including the length of the tail. The water they are kept in should be somewhat warmer than for some of the previous breeds mentioned: Don't let the water drop less than 50°F. Ideally, it should be kept somewhere between 65°F and 75°F.

Veiltails are not very competitive and should be kept only with other Veiltails. They are for a more experienced hobbyist. They are not for pond or outdoor use.

The Oranda is the result of crossing a Veiltail Goldfish with a Lionhead Goldfish. Some people call this breed the Fantailed Lionhead, because it looks as if it comes from Fantail stock, but this is a misnomer. In Japanese it is called the *oranda shishigashira,* which translated means "Rare Lionhead." The Calico Oranda is called *Azumanishiki.*

Like the Lionhead Goldfish (one of those without a dorsal fin), the Oranda has a bumpy growth over its head that resembles a wart. This high head growth, on good specimens, covers the head completely like a cap. This growth, however, should not cover the eyes, nostrils or mouth of the fish. The growth does not even begin to show until these fish are somewhere between two and three years old.

The Oranda body is egg-shaped and has long, flowing dual caudal and dual anal fins. The dorsal fin is the same as on a Veiltail.

Mostly available in the orange metallic variety, this head growth takes on the more concentrated coloration of orange. However, in nacreous coloration the growth may be white, orange, red, yellow, black, blue or calico. Again, the more blues and blacks, the more valuable the fish is thought to be. There is even a red cap or Tancho variety of Oranda, which is very striking and among the most highly prized, as its white body provides a stark contrast

21

This peculiar-looking fellow is known as a red-cap Oranda.

A Pearl-Scale Goldfish's scales give the impression of pearls sticking out of the fish's body.

to the bright cherry-red cap or hood that covers the head.

This fish has a life expectancy of approximately five to ten years, and should be kept at a relatively constant temperature somewhere around 65°F. Given enough room, an Oranda will grow to between 3 and 4 inches long, the length of the tail not included. Disease and fungus are sometimes a problem, as these tend to ferment in the folds and crevices of the cap. This fish should only be kept by someone who has experience with goldfish—it is definitely not for the beginner. The Oranda is not for a year-round outdoor pond.

This is a variety that is extremely popular. Essentially it looks like a Fantail, except that it is shorter and fatter, somewhat like a Ryukin, but with less exaggerated finnage. Its back arches high and its dorsal fin begins just forward of the peak of what looks like a hunchback. The abdomen protrudes much deeper than on almost any of the egg-shaped breeds, making the body large and ball-like. The caudal fin can sometimes develop into square veiltails.

The Pearl-Scale Goldfish is known for its odd scales, which seem almost spherical. There is a hard raised area in the center of each scale. These raised areas are usually white, and give the impression of pearls sticking out of the fish's body. The larger the scales, it is thought, the better the quality of the breed. An exceptional specimen will exhibit these scales all the way up the body to the dorsal fin. The scales, when they fall off from rubbing, fights or injury of any kind, grow back, but in a flat, normal variation. These "defects" are not passed on in breeding no matter when the injuries occur.

This fish has a life expectancy of approximately five to ten years, and should be kept at a relatively constant temperature somewhere between 55°F and 65°F, probably more toward the high end. Given enough room, a Pearl-Scale Goldfish will grow to be the size of a baseball or bigger, not including the fins. Disease and fungus are sometimes a problem, as these tend to ferment in the folds and crevices of the skin. Good filtration of the water is necessary to keep the fish healthy for some time.

The word *demekin* means "goldfish with the protruding eyes" in Japanese. This variety has been known in China since the

eighteenth century, according to the goldfish expert Marshall Ostrow, who claims that it was also known as the Dragon Fish or Dragon-eyed Goldfish. In England it is known as the Pop-eyed Goldfish. These Globe-eyed or Telescope-eyed Goldfish are known for their eyes, which protrude in almost tubelike fashion, in adults sometimes in lengths up to three quarters of an inch. The term "telescope" is an anomaly, since these fish have limited vision. There are four different eye shapes in the globe- or telescope-eyed varieties.

In body type and finnage—a short, round, egg-shaped body with double anal and caudal fins—they most resemble the Fantail. Their coloration ranges from orange metallic to nacreous, with combinations similar to those usually found

Goldfish with protruding eyes like the Telescope-eyed Goldfish have limited vision.

in Fantails. The matt version of these fish is extremely rare. There is a Veiltail version of the Telescope-eyed variety available as well.

This fish has a life expectancy of approximately five to ten years, and should be kept at a relatively constant temperature somewhere between 55°F and 65°F. You should probably err toward the warmer. Given enough room, a Telescope- or Globe-eyed Goldfish will grow to somewhere between 4 and 6 inches long, the length of the tail not included. Disease and fungus are sometimes a problem, as the eyes are very delicate and sensitive.

At an early age they do not have a problem with competition for food because their eyes have not yet begun to grow. However, as these fish get older (at around 6 months to 1 year in age), their eyes begin to protrude, limiting their vision and putting them at a disadvantage. It has been recommended that this type of fish be kept with its own kind or with other similarly handicapped fish. This fish should only be kept by someone who has experience with goldfish—it is definitely not for the beginner. These types of goldfish are not suitable for ponds.

The Black Moor is basically an all-black version of the Telescope- or Globe-eyed Goldfish. It is known solely for its color, which appears as a velvetlike black coat. The telescoped eyes are a little larger and

A Black Moor Goldfish has telescope eyes and appears to have a velvety coat.

The Bubble-eyed Goldfish has sacs around its eyes, which are prone to injury, but do repair them-selves. This exotic fish is an example of a dorsal-less gold-fish.

less prone to infection than the normal Telescope-eyed Goldfish.

Other than the Fantail, the Black Moor is the only round or egg-shaped goldfish that is hardy enough to survive in outdoor ponds, depending on where you live. Consult your local pet store owner. And, again, like the Fantail, the Black Moor does not make for a bad starter goldfish, because it is so hardy.

The Black Moor has a life expectancy of approximately five to ten years, and should be kept at a relatively constant temperature somewhere between 55°F and 65°F. You should probably err toward the

cooler. As Black Moors get older they develop a velvety texture. However, if the water is consistently too warm, orange will sometimes begin to show through. Once this happens, there is usually no going back. Given enough room, a Black Moor will grow to somewhere between 4 and 6 inches long, the length of the tail not included.

DORSAL-LESS GOLDFISH: THE EXOTICS

Dorsal-less goldfish are the final grouping of goldfish because they are the worst swimmers in the goldfish family. Without a dorsal fin, which is a stabilizing fin, it is

difficult for them to mount any
speed. They are not as fast, nor are
they as quick to turn, as even the
slow-moving Veiltails or the
Telescope- or Globe-eyed Goldfish.

This group tends to have
some of the most exotic of all the
goldfish and, as a result, many of
these are not recommended for
beginners. These fish require the
care and maintenance that are only
part of the experienced hobbyist's

knowledge. None of the fish in this
final group is suitable for outdoor
ponds or pools.

KOI

Koi come from a different species of
carp than the goldfish. Koi should
not be kept in small home aquariums with goldfish. Koi can grow to
over 3 feet in length in a large pond,
where they can be safely mixed with
large goldfish.

CHAPTER THREE

Choosing Your Goldfish

There are telltale signs you should look for when selecting your fish, no matter what variety. These tips should be strictly adhered to, as you do not want to buy a diseased fish right from the start. Never purchase new arrivals that have not been quarantined by the dealer.

SIGNS OF A HEALTHY GOLDFISH

ACTIVITY LEVEL—This is the most important thing to look for. You want healthy, active fish that swim smoothly, are capable of quick reactions and seem alert to their

When searching for your goldfish, look for healthy, active fish that swim smoothly and seem alert to their surroundings.

surroundings. You should not buy a fish that is either always at the top or the bottom of the tank, that is swimming on its side or that is upside down. Any fish that looks as though it's having trouble swimming should be avoided.

EYES—Never let someone sell you a fish that has cloudy eyes, cataracts, or any other kind of mutation of the eyes unless that person is an expert in that breed. A goldfish's eyes should be bright, clear and unclouded, and the fish should react to light.

FINS—Including the tail fin, the fish's fins should be erect or upright and intact. They should almost always be fanned out. You should not buy a fish with any spots of fungus anywhere on its fins, and there should be no frayed, split or folded surfaces.

SCALES—If there are any signs of fungus, white or otherwise, any wounds or any missing scales, don't buy the fish. Fish should have unblemished bodies, with no missing scales and no hints of disease.

ONE VARIETY OR A MIXTURE?

Generally speaking, goldfish are not aggressive when kept with other peaceful species. They, like all fish, tend to pick on injured or much smaller goldfish in the same tank, especially if they are crowded. Generally they are active and hardy fish, save a few of the more exotic species, like the Bubble Eyes, which require expert handling. In ponds or pools, like many fish, goldfish tend to school very easily. In these fish, there is never a lead goldfish—the school merely darts around following at whimsy one fish or another.

Remember, depending on what variety you decide on, you should keep them with other fish who have the same swimming ability, temperature and pH requirements, and temperament. For example, if you decided to raise Lionheads, you should not pair them with Comets. Comets are long, sleek and excellent swimmers. Lionheads are short and round and have no dorsal fins. The Comet is extremely hardy and competitive where food is concerned; the Lionhead is among the slowest of goldfish and would not do well paired with the Comet.

A Pearl-Scale Goldfish.

29

Lionheads are short and round and have no dorsal fins.

HOW TO AVOID OVERCROWDING

In order to avoid overcrowding, it is important to keep the proper number of fish for the number of gallons of water in your tank. You should use this information as a guide when setting up your aquarium with medium to large fancy goldfish. Remember, the amount of fish per tank depends on the size of the species you are keeping. Use common sense, and adjust your total number as required.

Gallons of Water	Number of Goldfish
10	1 or 2
20	2 or 3
30	3 or 4
55	6 or 7
70	9 or 10

Goldfish do tend to be aggressive during breeding time. However, there are no challenges or fights between males for the right to mate with a female goldfish. Male goldfish will merely chase any female down until they eventually get their chance to spawn.

Any good pet shop owner should tell you, when you are choosing fish, that goldfish should not be kept with tropical fish. Goldfish should be kept with goldfish. Why? There are many reasons.

MIXING OTHER SPECIES WITH GOLDFISH

Overall, the goldfish is a hardier species than other tropicals. Goldfish do not require a heater in their tank, and are actually better off if the temperature gets cold for a little while (six to eight weeks). Tropical fish, for the most part, require a consistent temperature, mostly in the mid- to high seventies, depending on the variety, while goldfish can live in the low fifties to mid-sixties. While the goldfish can survive in higher temperatures, they tend to develop some diseases more readily. The only species that should be kept with goldfish in a pond is koi. In an aquarium, goldfish can be kept with non-aggressive catfish and algae eaters.

Kept with cichlids, it is likely that your goldfish will be gone by morning. Even when kept only with other goldfish, it is important to keep the same types in groups together. Comets and Bubble Eyes would not be good together because the Comets swim faster and would tend to eat more and faster than the Bubble Eyes, which are delicate and need expert handling.

Lastly, given the opportunity, the goldfish will grow significantly larger than many other aquarium fish. There are exceptions, of course, including the Oscar and the Arrowana, both of which feed on small fish once they grow to a certain size.

AVOID OVERCROWDING

Goldfish are very hardy fish. They are generally very active and are capable of growing quite large. The common goldfish can grow to more than a foot long! The acknowledged rule for tropical fish is 1 inch of fish for each gallon of water. Most experts believe that each fancy goldfish should have 8 to 10 gallons of water to call its own. So, a 30 gallon tank would support three or four goldfish safely. If your goldfish become crowded, you will have to move them to a larger aquarium. This may seem excessive at first, but when they grow, you will quickly see

that it is very practical. A little common sense must be used at all times. When selecting the number of goldfish you want, you should keep in mind how big an aquarium you are choosing. This will determine the number (see "How to Avoid Overcrowding" sidebar).

Overcrowding will result in bad water conditions, and it will be difficult to supply adequate filtration in your tank for the number of fish. The idea is to create an environment that is beneficial to the fish, not to pack as many fish into as small a place as possible. The more space per goldfish, the healthier and more active they will be.

KEEPING THE BOTTOM OF THE TANK CLEAN

If you're wondering if you need a catfish to keep the bottom of your tank clean, the short answer is no. A small non-aggressive algae eater will help out quite a bit though. Goldfish are excellent bottom feeders, constantly scouting the aquarium floor for available food, but there are many particles that are too small for them to reach. Many tropical

Goldfish are excellent bottom feeders, constantly scouting the aquarium floor for food.

catfish are not able to withstand the colder temperatures goldfish prefer, so choose wisely. Cold, freshwater catfish are not a good idea since some have been known to suck the eyes out of the fancier goldfish varieties. No one knows why.

Do you need snails? Not really. Again, goldfish are excellent scavengers all by themselves. What do you need a snail for? You don't. Having snails in your aquarium will bring on more problems than it cures.

CHAPTER FOUR

A Home for Your Goldfish

There is no more popular an image than that of the goldfish swimming in the typical goldfish bowl. Ironically, there is nothing more harmful than placing a goldfish in this very inhumane contraption. While goldfish are extremely easy to care for, one of the things that must be guaranteed to them is well-aerated water. The goldfish bowl prevents this.

The typical goldfish bowl is wide in the middle and narrow up top. What you need is an aquarium or container that gives you maximum water surface-to-air ratios. The more water surface exposed to air, the more oxygen and gas will exchange, resulting in enough air for your goldfish to breathe comfortably.

For anyone who has had a goldfish in a goldfish bowl, the one thing you will remember is the goldfish near the surface of the water, breathing rather heavily. This is

because the goldfish was actually suffocating. The oxygen in the water had been quickly used up, leaving the fish no choice but to hang near the surface and gulp for air. This is not good for your fish. A muddy puddle in a deep pothole would probably be better.

In addition, a Common Goldfish will grow to 10 to 14 inches in length—but not in a bowl. You generally need 1 gallon of water for every inch of goldfish, unless you are purposely trying to dwarf your fish. What your goldfish needs is an aquarium.

FISH TANKS

Plastic tanks should be avoided, because they can melt under intense lighting. Plastic tanks also have a distorted view, and are too small to maintain a proper biological balance.

Many tanks today are made of glass and sealed with a silicone rubber cement that is both extremely strong and water-resistant. Never accept a tank that has any scratches on the glass or any spots that are not caulked with the silicone rubber cement. These tanks will have a tendency to either leak or burst.

Determine the size your goldfish will be at maturation and buy a tank to accommodate it.

The new acrylic tanks are much lighter than glass, have minimal distortion and come in a wide variety of shapes and sizes. Acrylic tanks scratch easily, so you should purchase a blemish remover kit along with the aquarium. Acrylic tanks are a little more expensive than glass, but are well worth the investment.

The first thing you need to remember when placing your tank on a surface is that it will be filled with water—*and water is heavy!* A fully loaded aquarium will weigh about 10 pounds per gallon. It is important that you use the strongest piece of furniture possible, or buy one of the specially constructed aquarium stands available at your local pet or department store.

WHERE DO I PUT THE AQUARIUM?

Whichever room you choose, never place the tank in front of a window. The result will be algae—and lots of it. While light is very necessary, placing the tank in front of a window will make for cleaning chores of the worst kind. Placing a tank near a window or door will make it susceptible to rapid temperature changes, which can be lethal.

WHAT IF I MUST USE A FISHBOWL?

If you must use a bowl, make sure that you select one of the smallest possible goldfish and choose the largest possible bowl. One beneficial item available for bowls is an under-gravel/bottom filter. The bases of these types of filters are round in shape and because of the air used to operate them, the water will be better aerated. However, it really is important, if you can, to get the biggest bowl possible, and to make sure it offers as great a surface area as possible. If you do use a bowl, the water should be changed frequently (at least 50 percent of the total volume each week).

WHAT ELSE DO I NEED TO KNOW WHEN I BUY A TANK?

When you buy a goldfish tank, buy an aquarium that will offer the greatest amount of surface area for gas exchange. Surface area refers to the part where the water meets the air. A deep 20-gallon tank will offer less surface area than a long 20-gallon tank. You don't particularly want to go deep. Generally it means that the water won't be especially well-aerated and it also means that it will be difficult to adjust things and to clean the tank because many things on the bottom will be more difficult to reach. Neither are the fish interested in going too deep. Goldfish would rather swim farther than deeper.

Shape is also important because the better aerated the water, the more fish you can comfortably house. A longer tank, with more surface area, offers the hobbyist the option of supporting more fish. Maybe only one or two, but that certainly is a big value to the beginner.

Surface area is an extremely important consideration for gas exchange when purchasing a tank. Note how much larger the surface-to-air ratio is for the tank vs. the bowl.

TANK SIZE

An important factor to consider when choosing your aquarium is the amount of free space that you will have available for your tank. If you live in a small apartment or house, a 10- or 20-gallon tank aquarium may be right for you. If you happen to live in a large home, you might be able to purchase a larger tank, such as a 40- or 55-gallon, without cramping your living space. The following table will give you a general idea of the minimum space requirements (length by width by height) that several standard size aquarium tanks will require.

10 Gallon

Regular	20 x 10 x 12
Long	24 x 8 x 12

15 Gallon

Regular	24 x 12 x 12
Long	20 x 10 x 18
Show	24 x 8 x 16

20 Gallon

High	24 x 12 x 16
Long	30 x 12 x 12

25 Gallon

Regular	24 x 12 x 20

30 Gallon

Regular	36 x 12 x 16
Breeding	36 x 18 x 12

40 Gallon

Long	48 x 13 x 16
Breeding	36 x 18 x 16

45 Gallon

Regular	36 x 12 x 24

50 Gallon

Regular	36 x 18 x 18

55 Gallon

Regular	48 x 13 x 20

65 Gallon

Regular	36 x 18 x 24

75 Gallon

Regular	48 x 18 x 20

SOCIAL CONSIDERATIONS

Family members and roommates should also be an important part of your placement decision. Even aquariums that are outfitted with state-of-the-art equipment are going to make some kind of noise. Most family members will probably find the sounds of an aquarium to be relaxing. But if you live with someone who would prefer not to continually listen to your aquarium, this may limit your placement options quite a bit.

NUMBER OF TANKS

When planning out your fishkeeping hobby, you must also decide if

FIVE STANDARD AQUARIUM SHAPES

Rectangle	Convex
Hexagon	Bubble
Octagon	

you are going to keep a single aquarium, or if you plan on expanding your hobby at a later date to accommodate more tanks. If you want to keep several different species of goldfish at one time, you might consider purchasing a few smaller tanks instead of buying just one large aquarium.

HOW MANY GALLONS DOES A TANK HOLD?

On some of the older tanks, it can be difficult to find information on exactly how many gallons the aquarium will hold. It is possible that you may run across one of these older tanks and would need to figure out how many gallons it holds. A good formula for obtaining gallon capacity of an aquarium is as follows:

$$\frac{Length \times Width \times Height}{231}$$

FIVE GOOD PLACES TO PURCHASE AQUARIUM EQUIPMENT

At a superstore

At a local pet shop

At a garage or estate sale

Through the want ads

From your friends

For example, a tank that measures 24 inches in length, by 12 inches in width, by 16 inches in height would contain approximately 20 gallons. This formula is very useful if you happen to run across a tank at a garage sale or auction.

BUYING USED TANKS

If you do decide to purchase a used tank, make sure to carefully inspect it for leaks, cracks and silicon wear. When buying used tanks from a retail dealer, check to see if the silicon seal is complete and uninterrupted. Even a small break in this seal can eventually lead to leaking. If the silicon is bad, remove it carefully with a razor and then replace it with new sealer. Allow the new sealer to

dry for at least 48 hours before you add any water to it.

TANK COVERS

The first things to buy for your tank are a cover and a light. The cover performs a number of functions. First, it stops unwanted objects from entering the tank and possibly injuring the fish. Second, it stops the fish from jumping out of the tank, as they sometimes want to do. Third, the cover stops splashes from affecting the carpeting, the hardwood floor or any valuable furniture near by. Fourth, it keeps the water from damaging the light over the tank. Fifth, it decreases evaporation.

If the cover is made of glass (many today are made of plastic), make sure that it is not too thin. It tends to get bumped and leaned on, or may need to support heavy objects—none of which is desirable, but which happens. A cheap, thin cover made of glass will easily break. A glass cover approximately $\frac{1}{8}$-inch thick should be fine. Never use a cover that does not fit correctly!

Whatever the cover, it should also provide you with easy access to the tank itself. Many are segmented in such a way that they have an area that lifts up so you don't have to remove the whole thing every time you feed your fish.

LIGHTS

Lighting is necessary both for illumination and to promote plant growth. Your pet shop is usually equipped with the various tubes or bulbs that are necessary to furnish your tank with light. The light is usually enclosed in a housing that sits on top of your cover.

Many lights today are fluorescent. These are cool and do not unnecessarily heat the water. They also tend to spread light more evenly and run on lower wattage than incandescent lights, which do not provide proper spectrums for aquarium purposes.

Actinic blue bulbs are good for plant growth because they produce long-wave ultraviolet radiation. Metal halide lights are expensive, but produce an effect that is very pleasing to the human eye. Mercury vapor lights are used for deeper tanks, and are usually suspended over the aquarium. These lights are expensive, but can retain up to 90 percent of their original capacity after a period of several years.

BUILDING YOUR OWN TANK

Do not try to build your own tank unless you really know how to make a secure and safe aquarium. Working with glass can be very dangerous. It is safer to purchase a tank from a reputable dealer than risk water leaks and other such disasters that often accompany aquariums that have been built by inexperienced hobbyists.

This Lionhead Goldfish is healthy thanks to the proper care of its aquarium.

39

The pet shop where you buy your lighting will be able to supply you with the proper bulbs for the lighting you choose. You need to know how long your tank is so that you can calculate the wattage necessary to illuminate the tank properly.

The rule is generally 2 to 2.5 watts per gallon of water. A 10-gallon tank would then require 20 to 25 watts of light from the lamp above. Again, this should be well distributed by the lamp and should extend the entire length of the tank.

HEATERS

Welcome to the world of the cold-water aquarist. Because you are choosing goldfish, you do not absolutely need to have an aquarium heater. The hardier strains of gold-fish, as has already been discussed, can generally withstand temperatures almost down to freezing. Some of the other varieties are less hardy, but can easily withstand temperatures in the low 60°F range, which is low enough to kill most tropical fish strains.

Provided you live in a warm climate or have heating in your home, there is normally no need for a heater in your aquarium. However, the smaller the tank, the more quickly the temperature may change. It is for this reason that many people have heaters. In an extremely hot climate, a chiller may be needed.

Having a heater is a wise precaution. It will keep your aquarium at a constant temperature and make your

Goldfish can withstand temperatures almost down to freezing.

life a little easier. Thermostat heaters are usually submersible, and have external controls. The thermostat can be set or reset at any time. A pilot or warning light usually lets you know that the heater is on. Never, ever pull your heater out of the water while it is on, as this is a good way to ruin your thermostat and cause the tube housing the heating element to shatter or explode! Unplug your heater for 20 minutes before removing it from the aquarium.

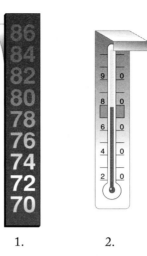

1.　　　　2.

Examples of thermometers: (1) A digital thermometer that attaches on the outside of the aquarium. (2) A metal thermometer; this type attaches to the side of the aquarium and hangs in the water.

THERMOMETERS

You need a thermometer to monitor the temperature of the water. There are two types of thermometers that are popular. The first is the internal floating thermometer. The second is the external stick-on thermometer. The external thermometers can be difficult to see in low light levels, cannot be easily removed once they are applied, and tend to read a bit low—probably 2°F—so keep that in mind.

FILTERS

There are six basic types of filters: box filters, which go inside the tank;

power filters, which go outside the tank; undergravel filters, which lay beneath the substrate; canister filters, which hang on the tank or sit on the floor; fluidized bed filters, which hang on the tank; and sponge filters, which sit in the aquarium. The box filter, power filter and canister filter have a series of layers of wadding, charcoal and other media to remove debris and chemicals from the water, while the under gravel filter uses the substrate to create a natural filter. The sponge filter provides a surface area for bacteria to colonize, and the fluidized bed filter uses sand as a biological medium.

Let's discuss first what the filter does. The filter has two or three

BRINGING YOUR GOLDFISH HOME

When you bring home your goldfish, your pet dealer will have put the fish in clear plastic baggies filled with water and enough oxygen for a short trip. Ask to have this plastic bag placed in another bag—a paper bag or a dark opaque plastic bag, if possible. The first thing you must do is resist the temptation to take the fish out in the light and gawk at it. Bringing the fish from the dark into the light and then back to dark will put the fish into shock. This weakens the fish and its resistance to other possible maladies. Keep it in the bag until you get home.

ostensible purposes, depending on what kind you use. First, it cleanses and purifies the water through the use of a biological colony and chemical reactions. Second, it circulates the water. Third, in most cases, it aerates the water.

Because goldfish emit an exceeding large amount of ammonia, you will need at least two filtration units on your system at all times. A power filter combined with an undergravel filter will provide the essential biological, mechanical and chemical filtration that is required to maintain a healthy system.

What You Should Know About Power Filters

These filters hang on the outside of the tank, usually in the back of the tank so as not to interfere with the view. Usually they are powered by their own motor; however, there are some that will use an air pump to power them. Water passes from the tank through an upside-down U-shaped tube into the filter. Air comes from a tube, which is attached to the top of the filter leading out of the tank. This is attached to an air pump. As the air races through the filter, that water is pushed out, drawing in more water through small slits on the top of the filter. There it goes through the same series of wadded media as in the box filter before it is pumped back out into the tank.

AIR PUMPS

Depending on what kind of filter you decide to use, you can then decide what size air pump you need. If you choose an outside or power filter, you need only a small pump to use for an airstone or other device to supply more oxygen to the water.

There are two basic kinds of pumps: diaphragm pumps, which

have a vibrating rubber diaphragm, and piston pumps. Both are solid additions to any aquarium; however, while the diaphragm types require no attention, piston pumps do require oiling occasionally. Piston pumps tend to deliver more power, though. Air pumps may generate some noise, so quietness is a special sales feature aside from strength, when choosing the right one for you. Pumps are made to support anything from a large bowl to a slew of tanks. Talk to your pet professional regarding your specific tank.

AERATION

Goldfish need a lot of oxygen in the water. Airstones help to supply extra oxygen saturation.

Airstones are generally made of porous rock attached at the end of an air hose. The stone gives off tiny bubbles, which aerate the water. You don't want too fine a mist—tiny bubbles are best. Other air releasers are usually made of plastic and are weighted at the bottom. They come as sunken treasure chests, fallen barrels, old-fashioned underwater divers—there's an amazing assortment to choose from. Remember,

you don't want big bubbles racing to the surface. You want a steady stream of medium-sized bubbles that take their time going upward, giving them a chance to add oxygen to the water.

These are very important features of any aquarium setup, and it is strongly recommend that you have at least one air-release device in a 10- or 20-gallon tank, and at least two in a 30-gallon tank or larger.

OTHER ACCESSORIES

There are any number of accessories available for aquariums. Listed below are some of the more important ones.

Gravel should be no smaller or finer than medium coarse so that it is not accidentally ingested, and it should be smooth so that it does not damage the fishes' mouths.

44

AIR HOSES—Sold at pet stores, this plastic tubing will enable you to attach your air pump to the filter and/or aeration devices. Air hoses should snugly fit all joints and no air should escape anywhere. If there is air leakage, the resultant loss of pressure more often than not will cause the filter not to live up to its potential or possibly cause your air pump to burn out faster.

AIR VALVES—Air valves enable the aquarist to run additional aeration or filter devices off a single pump. A single pump should be able to supply a filter and an aeration device. An air valve takes the feed from the air pump and then distributes it to two, three, four or more valves which can be used or shut off in case of non-use. This allows you to send pumped air to different devices in different parts of the tank. It also allows you to control the air flow to these different places.

ALGAE SPONGE OR AQUARIUM CLEANER—This is a sponge that is usually attached to a long handle and is used for scraping down the inside of the tank without having to empty it out. This can be done while the fish are still in the tank. It is

good for removing algae that have grown on the inside walls of the tank. The sponge is strong enough to scrape off algae but will not scratch the glass.

AQUARIUM SCREENS OR BACKGROUNDS—Aquarium screens are placed on the outside of the tank, facing the front of the tank. The idea is to hide the tubing, filters, pumps, etc., that are usually kept at the back of the aquarium, and provide an extra sense of security for your fish. Aquaria most often are placed against a wall. Aquarium screens prevent you from seeing the wallpaper or paint on the wall behind the tank, since many times these wall colorings are not especially a part of the natural habitat of goldfish.

FISHNET—This is an important piece of equipment. The fishnet should not be too small (leaving you too small an area with which to catch your fish) or too big (making it difficult to maneuver inside your tank and around the various rocks, plants, etc.). You will use this more than you think. You will need it when you have to take out an ailing or dead fish, or an aggressive fish, and when you need to take out all the fish to clean the aquarium. Keep a variety of nets on hand, in case of an emergency.

VACUUMS—There are such things as aquarium vacuums. These are usually small hand-pump, gravity flow or electrically powered siphons that extract larger debris from the aquarium floor. Especially with goldfish, these are quite handy. They perform a very necessary task in helping to clean your tank and maintain a debris-free environment.

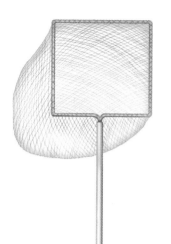

You will use your fishnet frequently.

45

GRAVEL

Gravel is an important consideration in setting up any fish tank, but especially so with goldfish. Goldfish are excellent scavengers and bottom feeders. They will take up big bunches of gravel, hold them in their mouths and then spit them back out. Goldfish are also known for moving gravel around quite a bit. Gravel should be naturally colored, and of smooth contour to avoid damage to your goldfish's mouth.

AQUASCAPING

In general, aquascaping means setting up the inside of the tank so that it is pleasing to the human eye as well as pleasing to the fish. Aquascaping includes the placement of rocks, air releases, plants and any wood pieces you've decided to include. The concept is to set up something resembling a natural habitat. I will discuss whether to have real rocks, wood or plants instead of fake ones later in the book. Let me deal with the layout now; you can decide later if it will be filled with living materials or artificial decorations.

Where you have placed your aquarium will dictate how you should aquascape it. If it can only be viewed from the front, then you should plan to aquascape for a frontal view. However, if the aquarium can be approached from many different angles, then those angles need to be addressed as well.

Some people make a rough sketch of what they would like, or find a photograph of what they would like to do. It is advisable to have a solid idea of what you want before you go into the store. By understanding what you want, you can plan better when it comes to terracing your gravel, and placing large stones or logs which will hide tubing and filters, etc. Depending

on the plants you choose, need to be bunched togeth others will need to be alone. aquarists tend to place their plants toward the back of the If you want an aquarium scree this should also be taken into account when deciding on your aquascaping.

As far as plants go, never have even numbers, as that symmetry in nature mostly does not exist. Place the smaller plants and objects up front. Also, land rocks are not as good as rocks taken from ponds. Land rocks tend to be jagged and could injure your fish. Rocks found

Think about how you'd like your aquarium to look before you start aqua-scaping. This fish swims by an Echinodorus bleheri *plant.*

in streams and ponds tend to be rounded and are better for fish. Of all rocks, shale and slate tend to be the best. Driftwood is a nice touch, but make sure to have driftwood that is weighted down. It is best to buy this from a pet store, so that it is guaranteed to be properly cured for your goldfish.

Don't place too many objects in the tank—don't overaquascape. Make sure to leave an area open for swimming. This is generally called the swimming space. Fish like to have a place to hide, especially in the plants you have supplied, but they need a place to swim and exert themselves as well. It is usually best if this is left open up front, so that you can view the fish when they are most active.

It is true of rocks and wood that these are best when purchased through pet stores, so as to avoid any problems of toxic properties that might contaminate the water and fish. If you must use rocks from around your home, it is a good idea to steam-clean them first. Never place seashells or any marine or sea life in with your goldfish. These are not freshwater items and will cause the water to become much too alkaline for your fish.

IF YOUR GOLDFISH GETS GRAVEL STUCK IN ITS MOUTH

Goldfish sometimes get bits of gravel caught in their mouths. Usually this will dislodge itself over a matter of several hours without damage to the fish. However, in those cases where the gravel does not dislodge, attempt the following, recommended by the Goldfish Society of America in its *Official Guide to the Goldfish:*

1. Capture the fish with a fishnet.

2. Hold the fish head down and press against both sides of the lips, opening the mouth.

3. With your other hand, press the throat behind the stone. Relief is usually immediate.

SETTING UP YOUR AQUARIUM

Follow these recommended steps to set up your aquarium.

1. Thoroughly rinse your aquarium with clean water. Set the undergravel filter in place. In a separate container, wash the gravel. Do not use soap of any kind. Empty the gravel into a container, fill it up with water and then

dump the water and start all over again. You must agitate the gravel during each rinse by moving the gravel around while submerged to get the dirt and other toxic debris off the gravel. Generally, for brand-new gravel, four or five thorough rinsings are enough. Don't skimp on this step, as uncleaned gravel will not only make for cloudy water, but water unsafe for your goldfish.

2. Make sure the tank is exactly where you want it to be. You should not move the tank once you begin to fill it. (Tanks are not made for movement once they have been filled.) Pour the gravel gently into the tank. The gravel should slope uphill toward the back of the tank. The gravel layer in the front should be 2 inches in depth, and gently rise to a 2½-inch depth in the rear. Begin the aquascaping of your tank (add any large pieces now—rocks, pieces of wood, etc. All these should be thoroughly rinsed off before being put into the tank. Again, don't use soap in cleaning anything—just clear water). Do not set rocks against the tank walls or directly on the filter

plates which can cause dead spots in the undergravel filtration.

3. If you have an airstone or air release, put it in place now.

4. Add the water to the tank. Use tap water. The container to carry water from the tap to the aquarium should be free of any soap or other element that would dirty the water. It is best, if you have a large piece in the tank, to pour the water on it, trying not to disturb your aquascape too much. After water is added, you may need to re-aquascape.

5. Place the power filter on the back of the aquarium and the heater inside of the tank.

6. Place the plants in the gravel. If you are using live plants, remember to weight them down (see Chapter 6 for more information on live plants). Place the thermometer in now as well.

7. Plug all of the equipment in after you have set it up and hooked up all the hoses. Turn the equipment on. Make sure the heater is properly adjusted and that the filter is working. Add a dechlorinator to remove chlorine and chloramines from the water.

You can create water that is suitable for any type of fish.

8. After the tank has run for 24 hours, you should check and adjust the temperature hardness and pH levels before adding any fish!

9. Add a few starter fish (guppies or feeder goldfish work great) to begin the nitrogen cycle. Leave them in the aquarium until cycling is complete (about three weeks), then add a few more fancy goldfish every other week until capacity is reached.

THE WATER

Goldfish, even the exotics, tend to be hardy. However, it is important to be able to control the water, because there are a number of things that influence fish where water is concerned.

There are two water-quality parameters a goldfish enthusiast should continually watch: hard as opposed to soft water and acidity versus alkalinity. Before you place your goldfish in the aquarium, make sure to test the water for both.

HARDNESS—Hardness refers to the amount of salts, namely calcium and magnesium, in the water. Water that lacks salts is referred to as soft. Hardness can be dealt with in a number of ways. While goldfish can survive generally hard water, there is no need to place your fish at risk. A water-hardness test and correction kits can be purchased at your local pet store. Golfish do well in slightly hard water conditions (9 to 12dH).

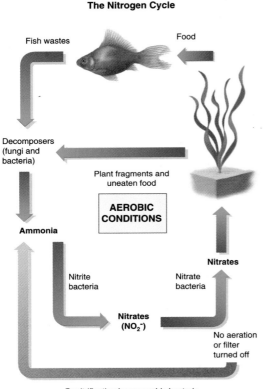

The Nitrogen Cycle

Fish wastes

Food

Decomposers
(fungi and
bacteria)

Plant fragments and
uneaten food

**AEROBIC
CONDITIONS**

Ammonia

Nitrates

Nitrite
bacteria

Nitrate
bacteria

**Nitrates
(NO₂⁻)**

No aeration
or filter
turned off

Denitrification by anaerobic bacteria
ANAEROBIC CONDITIONS

between 7.2 and 7.6. This can be determined by using a pH test kit, which can be purchased at all pet shops.

NITRATES—Another problem in goldfish tanks is that of the nitrogen cycle. Fish wastes, uneaten foods and plant fragments decay and break down into ammonium compounds. Ammonia is not good for your fish. Natural bacteria *(nitrosomonas)* that grow in the aquarium convert these ammonium compounds into nitrites. Nitrites are not good for your goldfish either, although they are less harmful than ammonia. A second type of bacteria *(nitrobacter)* which also grow naturally in all aquaria turn these nitrites into nitrates. Goldfish cannot withstand great amounts of nitrates without too many problems. Plants, however, use nitrates and give off oxygen in return. Frequent water changes will also lower the nitrate level.

Since all of this happens naturally, you might think that there's nothing to worry about. Wrong! In new aquariums many beginners experience "new tank syndrome." New tank syndrome is when all your new fish die because the nitrogen

PH—pH refers to the amount of acidity in the water. Neutral water has a pH of 7. Acidic water has a pH less than 7 and alkaline water has a pH greater than 7. The more acidic, the lower the pH, and the more alkaline, the higher the pH. Goldfish hobbyists should maintain their aquarium's pH somewhere

cycle was not properly completed. Don't fall victim to this. The bacteria populations that build in your tank can take anywhere from two to four months to establish themselves, depending on certain conditions. Ammonia, nitrite and nitrate test kits are available and are invaluable when starting up a new aquarium.

PLACING THE FISH IN THE TANK

It is important to follow the steps described below. While goldfish are a hardy breed, they are not the best travelers, and tend to go into shock during transportation and introduction into a new tank.

1. When you get home, take the plastic baggies of fish and place them in the tank without opening them. This helps to allow the temperature in the bag to acclimate to the temperature of the tank. Let it sit for ten minutes.

2. Open the bag and let air get in it. Take a handful of water from the tank and pour it into the bag. Let this stand for another ten or fifteen minutes. Repeat until the original amount of water in the bag has doubled.

3. Lift the bag out of the aquarium and discard half to two-thirds of the water in the bag (you don't want to dump a lot of water from someone else's aquarium into your own). Place a fishnet in front of the bag just to make sure the fish don't accidentally swim out. Pour some more water from your aquarium into the bag and let it sit for another five to ten minutes.

4. Place the bag back in the aquarium, and tilt it so that your fish can swim out on their own.

Note: It is important to know that you really should buy and introduce into the aquarium all your goldfish within three to six weeks of each other. Introducing a new goldfish much later, after the fish have already set up certain patterns, may result in aggressive behavior, disrupting the tank. All the fish should be of approximately the same size and age.

CHAPTER FIVE

Aquarium Maintenance

The two most important things to do with an already operating fish tank are two of the most enjoyable. First, turn the aquarium light on and off every day. Light is important both for the fish and the

plants. They should receive at least eight hours of light per day. Second, remember to feed your fish every day. You need to do this at the same spot of the tank each time and around the same time each morning, afternoon and night. The most important thing that any fish hobbyist can do, other than these two things, is be observant. You must closely watch the fish for signs of disease and watch their interaction to see if any are being picked on by the rest. You must check the plants to see if any parts of them are dying; if they are, these brown sections must be removed at once. You must check the water temperature to make sure that it remains constant.

A responsible owner makes every effort to provide a clean environment that fish will thrive in.

You need to examine the airstone, the filter and the heater to make sure they are all in working order. Make sure that all equipment is operating at maximum efficiency.

GENERAL MAINTENANCE

Cleaning a fish tank involves elbow grease. In fact, maintaining a fish tank is not for the lazy at heart. Concern must be shown at every step and every level. Your fishes' lives depend on your attention to detail.

Vacuuming

Vacuuming is one of the most important parts of maintaining your tank. You must prevent the buildup of mulm in the gravel. Mulm is a combination of fish wastes, plant fragments and uneaten food that decay at the bottom of your tank. It is very important to clean this up because it creates biological problems. It also clogs up the filters and builds up on the gravel.

Vacuuming is important even if you have an undergravel filter because you don't want the mulm getting caught in the gravel and preventing a flow of water through the filter plate. Powerheads can be added to the uplift tubes to increase circulation.

Check the Filter

Remember to check the power or canister or box filter's medium. The top-level mat gets dirty quickly and easily, as this is the stage that collects the largest pieces of debris. If there is a buildup in your box, canister or power filter here, it will reduce the flow of water through the filter and reduce the filter's effectiveness.

Corner filter mat should be replaced when it is dirty. Rinse a power or canister filter's mat off with clear water periodically. Replace it when it becomes clogged. There are certain bacteria that build up in your filter that are beneficial to the filtering process. A good rinse is satisfactory in most cases.

Scrape Algae

Another important thing to do is algae scraping. Algae are the soft brown, blue-green or red plant life that develop all over your tank. They develop faster in some tanks than in others, depending on your tank's proximity to real sunlight, oxygen saturation and excess amounts of food in the tank. Algae scrapers are either sponges attached to a long stick or are a pair of magnetized scrapers that will help you to clean the inside of the aquarium walls so that you can see better inside. It is important to stop too much algae growth. At lower levels, algae perform the same beneficial tasks that all plants do. However, algae can overrun your tank.

Never use soap to clean anything in your tank. Water and elbow grease are always the best weapons against dirt and algae.

It is important to clean away the surface film of algae. Here, a magnetic scraper is used.

Test the Water

Water testing is very important. For the first month, check the water twice a week. After that, there will be sufficient bacteria buildup for you to have what is known as a mature tank. After this takes place, you can reduce your testing to once a week.

WATER CHANGES

A water change is when you literally take out a quarter, a third or half of the existing water and replace it with distilled water. The amount you change is up to you, depending on the water quality of your tank. A 20 to 25 percent weekly change is recommended for most goldfish aquariums. Water changes are one of the most important aspects of cleaning and maintaining your tank. Goldfish are messy fish in many instances, and so water maintenance is important.

Water changes go a long way toward maintaining good water quality. Water changes are also beneficial because you can dilute the amount of ammonia, nitrites and nitrates in the water, as well as other harmful gases and substances, and the water you add will be more

Siphoning: Step 1

Siphoning: Step 2

oxygen-rich than water that has been in your tank for some time. Water changes will also replace important trace elements that have been lost.

Change the water after you have cleaned everything else. To do this, you must first siphon water off so that you can later add new water. To siphon water without a hand pump or electrically driven unit, you need a long (3 feet), thick tube or a hand-pump siphon, and a large bucket.

How to Siphon with a Standard Tube

1. Fill the tube up with water until it's ready to overflow at both ends, making sure there is no trapped air anywhere in the tube. Place your thumbs over the ends of the tube on either side.

2. With your thumbs still holding the water in, place one end of the tube in the tank and aim the

other end of the tube at the bucket. Make sure the bucket is lower than the tank or siphoning will not work.

3. Release your thumbs and the water will begin to flow.

Some hobbyists use the siphon to vacuum the bottom of the tank. This kills two birds with one stone. Either way, you must do both. Make sure that the water you add to your tank is not straight from the faucet, but, rather, has been aged at least twenty-four to forty-eight hours. Either keep a bunch of 1-gallon jugs stored somewhere in the house, or make sure to keep a 5-gallon bucket somewhere that has been filled with water for several days. Clean plastic milk jugs (with the caps off) work well for storing water.

WATER CHANGERS

There are devices that can be hooked up to your tank that will change the water for you on a constant basis. Whether you have chlorinated water or not, your local pet shop will be able to fit you with one of these, should you want one. It

A water changer can be used to siphon and to refill the tank to maintain acceptable water conditions.

makes life much easier but requires that you have a faucet constantly available somewhere relatively near your aquarium. Water changers are great laborsaving devices and make maintenance that much easier and life better for your fish.

MAINTENANCE CHECKLISTS

Daily

- Feed the goldfish twice a day and check their physical condition.

- Turn the tank lights on for eight hours per day.

- Check the water temperature.

- Make sure the filters are still in working order.

- Make sure the pumps are providing maximum output.

Weekly

- Study the fish for diseases by observing them closely in the tank.

- Change approximately 20 to 25 percent of the aquarium water.

ONE-YEAR CLEANING CYCLE

January	Monthly
February	Monthly
March	**Quarterly**
April	Monthly
May	Monthly
June	**Quarterly**
July	Monthly
August	Monthly
September	**Quarterly**
October	Monthly
November	Monthly
December	**Yearly**

- Add distilled water to make up for any evaporated water loss.

- Check the filter to see if the top mat needs to be rinsed or replaced.

- Vacuum the tank thoroughly, and attempt to clean up all mulm.

- Test the water for pH, ammonia, nitrates and hardness.

- Trim any brown portions of live plants.

This fish doesn't know it, but it takes a caring hobbyist to keep its aquarium water fresh and clean.

Monthly

- Change another 25 percent of the water; replace with distilled water.

- Clean the tank's glass on inside using an algae scraper.

- Vacuum the tank thoroughly, stirring up the gravel and eliminating mulm.

- Trim any brown portions of plants and replace them if necessary.

- Wash off any tank decorations that suffer from dirt buildup.

Quarterly

- Change 50 percent of the water; replace with distilled water.

- Replace the airstones.

- Rinse the filter materials completely and change them if necessary.

- Wash the gravel in really dirty places.

- Clean the glass on the inside using an algae scraper.

- Vacuum the tank thoroughly, stirring up the gravel and eliminating mulm.

- Trim any brown portions of plants and replace them if necessary.
- Wash off any decorations that suffer from dirt buildup.

Yearly

- Do a total strip-down; replace the filter medium with new matt and charcoal.
- Replace the airstones.
- Wash the gravel entirely.
- Clean the inside of the tank thoroughly. Start up all over again.

FIVE HANDY AQUARIUM GADGETS

Algae scraper

Scrub brush

Cable caddy

Siphon hose

Plastic buckets

CHAPTER SIX

Plants—Living or Artificial?

The one thing goldfish fanciers all know, though some would not like to admit it, is that goldfish are not especially kind to live plants. In most cases, goldfish treat plants the way we do potato chips—they munch on 'em.

Many experienced goldfish hobbyists know that keeping live plants with goldfish requires equal care for the plants and for the fish themselves. It can be done, but it requires work and constant attention. You should consider how much time you want to devote to your fish tank before you decide on artificial or live plants. There are many goldfish experts who do not keep goldfish with either gravel or plants, but that's not aesthetically pleasing or

Live plants are an excellent source of oxygen, but some species can be difficult for novice aquarists.

beneficial to your fish's feelings of security.

There are a great number of artificial plants to choose from, and many of the better-made ones look like the real thing. Most of the better artificial plant manufacturers provide replicas of all the plants described in this chapter. Avoid using unnatural colored artificial plants, which will distract from the beauty of your goldfish.

WHY LIVE PLANTS?

First of all, live plants provide an excellent source of oxygen as a result of photosynthesis. Plants absorb carbon dioxide and the nitrates that naturally occur in your fish tank that might become a serious problem if there is too much buildup. They provide shade and hiding, egg-laying sites and food for your goldfish. Some experienced goldfish keepers

FIVE REASONS TO KEEP LIVE PLANTS

Plants give off oxygen

Plants absorb carbon dioxide

Plants remove nitrates

Plants provide shelter

Plants provide spawning grounds

plant two different types of plants in their aquariums: the tough plants that cannot be so easily eaten by goldfish and smaller, more tender plants that are stocked purposely to be eaten. The latter group is provided so that the former group might grow more successfully.

Plant Types

There are three major types of plants: rooted, bunches and floaters. *Rooted* plants usually grow in numbers, but separate from one another. *Bunches* are plants that quickly reproduce off one stem, and can quickly envelop a tank. *Floaters* are floating plants whose root system dangles in the water. These usually grow near the surface, or in some cases, right out of the water. Each of these groups will provide two or

three varieties that can survive goldfish.

If you choose live plants, please follow this advice. Always buy plants from a reputable dealer. Pick no more than two or three types of plant—two is preferable. Pay attention to these sets of plants and learn how to deal with them as best you can. The simpler you keep it, the faster and better you will learn to grow and keep plants. *Sagittaria (Sagittaria graminea)* and *elodea (Anacharis canadensis)* are hardy and hard to kill and are recommended to novices. Don't feel bad or give up if you kill the first set of plants— eventually you'll master this difficult phase of aquarium maintenance.

PLASTIC OR REAL?

For the beginner, understanding how an aquarium works and the attention needed to run it successfully need to be learned before becoming a freshwater botanist, so it is recommended to start off with plastic plants. There is nothing worse than having to scoop up the brown remains of what used to be plant life in your new aquarium. It is better to learn how your fish react to so many different disturbances and how to deal with the many other issues of aquarium maintenance before learning how to grow plants successfully and how to defend them from your goldfish.

ROOTED PLANTS

There are three types of rooted plants that you should consider planting with goldfish: *Sagittaria (Sagittaria graminea), Vallisneria (Vallisneria spiralis)* and the Amazon Sword Plant *(Echinodorus*

grandiflorus). These do not appeal to goldfish as much as other plants might. But make no mistake, gold-fish will eventually, if they have a mind to, destroy almost any plant.

These plants should be pruned whenever there is brown found on any part of them. Decay on most freshwater aquatic plants must be clipped off immediately, before it kills the plant itself.

SAGITTARIA—These plants can grow up to 36 inches in height.

These fish are in front of the Aponogeton undulatus, *a rooted plant.*

FIVE AQUASCAPING MATERIALS

Marble rock

Shale rock

Igneous rock

Stratified rock

Driftwood

With long, straight leaves, they are best when placed in bunches. They are generally sturdy plants. These plants can survive in temperatures as high as 77°F, but they are also hardy cold-water plants and do not require a lot of light to thrive.

VALLISNERIA SPIRALIS—Again, these are pretty hardy plants. *Vallisneria* has long, ribbonlike leaves that spiral upward. It looks like a curly version of *Sagittaria* and will grow approximately 2 feet long. These plants are not quite as hardy as *Sagittaria,* as they have a more delicate temperature zone ranging from 59°F to 72°F.

AMAZON SWORD PLANT—The Amazon Sword Plant may have as many as thirty to forty leaves growing from it. The leaves are broad in the middle and tapered at each end.

There is also a broad-leafed Amazon sword plant. This plant does well in medium to strong sunlight, or, alternatively, it should get approximately eight to ten hours of electric light a day. It can survive in temperatures up to 80°F.

BUNCHED PLANTS

Elodea *(Anacharis canadensis)* and milfoil *(Myriophyllum aquaticum)* are similar and offer the aquarist more than enough choices to make the aquascape interesting and healthy in their tanks.

Bunched plants are plants that propagate by way of cuttings. You buy cuttings from your pet dealer, slice off the bottom inch and, on the next inch, take off many of the leaves. Weight down the bunch and plant the plucked inch into the gravel. These plants will take hold quickly and grow just as fast. Don't buy any plant that is already browning, as it will shortly be dead. Buy only solidly green specimens.

Pondweed *(Elodea canadensis)* is a favorite for cold freshwater tanks. Pondweed is long, with narrow stalks that sprout rings of thick green leaves. In a regular tank these plants would need constant pruning. That may or may not be the case in your goldfish tank. However, they grow fast and can sometimes outgrow even a school of goldfishes' hunger.

Elodea is reproduced by cutting off the lower inch when you buy it from your pet store and planting the remainder firmly in the gravel. They should be weighted. Generally speaking, they usually root pretty quickly and are very hardy. They can withstand temperatures up to approximately 80°F.

Milfoil *(Myriophyllum aquaticum),* commonly called foxtail, is another favorite in freshwater tanks. Given strong light, Milfoil can sometimes grow three to four inches in a week's time. They look much like elodea, except that they sprout much finer leaves, like eyelashes, in rings around the stalk. Otherwise, much of what goes for elodea also holds true for Milfoil.

FLOATING PLANTS

Floating plants are highly recommended for goldfish, but, unfortunately, for outdoor ponds only. These plants require great

This Anachris plant is an example of a bunch plant.

Floating plants like this Water Sprite are fast-growing and thought to block light needed by other plants.

amounts of strong sunlight and generally grow much too large for aquarium use. While they have been grown and maintained by experts, it is not recommended even for journeymen aquarists. If your heart is set on floating plants, however, discuss options with your pet dealer.

OTHER PLANTS OF INTEREST

There are several other plants that do well with your goldfish in a cold-water aquarium and they include:

1. Japanese Dwarf Rush *(Acorus gramineus)*—a short shrub-like plant.

2. Baby's Tears *(Bacopa monnieria)*—which needs strong lighting.

3. Hornwort *(Ceratophyllum demersum)*—not easily eaten by fish.

4. Hairgrass *(Eleocharis acicularis)*—which requires good lighting.

5. Willowmoss *(Fontinalis antipyretica)*—attaches to rocks.

6. Java Moss *(Vesicularia dubyana)*—attaches on rocks.

CHAPTER SEVEN

Positively Nutritious

WHAT DO I FEED MY GOLDFISH?

Omnivores are animals that eat both meat and vegetable matter on a regular basis. Omnivore is a very good classification for goldfish, because they eat everything. Flake foods in general supply goldfish with a very balanced diet. These foods are well designed to provide goldfish with the essentials necessary for a long and happy life. There are, however, other types of food. Goldfish eat red worms, whiteworms, earthworms and tubifex. They will eat brine shrimp, mosquito larvae and fruit flies. They love almost any kind of seafood—crab, lobster, clams—either fresh or canned. They can also

TYPES OF FISH

There are three types of fish: carnivores, herbivores and omnivores. Carnivores only eat other fish or live food. Piranhas, for example, only eat other fish or other animals. Many fish enthusiasts actually feed common goldfish to piranhas. They will also eat hamburger, bits of luncheon meat and an assortment of other solid or table foods, which they tear apart with their teeth. Herbivores eat only vegetable matter. They will eat flake foods and many types of vegetable matter, including the plants in your tank. An excellent example of a herbivore is an Angelfish. Goldfish are omnivores. They will eat flakes, live food and bits of table food. Basically, they will eat almost anything; however, they rarely eat anything as large as another fish in the same way an adult piranha or Oscar will.

be fed canned foods, such as canned vegetables—beans are especially good for them. Fresh spinach, broccoli and cauliflower are also excellent additions. You can use flake foods as your goldfish's staple food, but you should make an attempt to substitute other foods several times a week to ensure the best possible results. Live foods and vegetables can quickly foul the water, so feed them to your fish sparingly.

Food Categories

The following is a breakdown, food by food, of what you might feed your fish. There are basically four different food categories: flake or dried foods; frozen or freeze-dried foods; live foods; and table scraps or household foods.

FLAKES OR DRIED FOODS

There are numerous manufacturers of flake or dried foods, and these foods are available in a wide variety of shapes and sizes. Some fish food manufacturers produce flake and dried foods especially for goldfish, which address their unique nutritional requirements.

Many dried food manufacturers have begun marketing feeding kits that promise to improve growth and color. The results are mixed, but one thing is for sure. Don't buy these kits unless they are exclusively aimed at goldfish. If a particular type of food is aimed at tropical fish in general, it is probably not a good buy for goldfish. Goldfishes' nutritional needs differ greatly from community or incompatible tropical fish, and the results will not be satisfactory.

LIVE FOODS

Given the best of all possible scenarios, live food is easily the best food to give as a treat to your always hungry goldfish. The problem is that these foods stand the chance of being laden with disease.

Live foods can easily be obtained in small quantities from your local pet store, and can usually be bought in one- or two-serving sizes. The live food you get at your local pet store is, to a great degree, safe because it has probably been cultivated in a hatchery.

The only two live foods that generally do not run the risk of carrying a disease are earthworms and brine shrimp. Both brine shrimp and earthworms are easily obtained, and are an excellent addition to your fishes' diet.

Note: No matter what any expert tells you, never go searching in lakes or ponds for live foods. Since most of these are larvae, they tend to be in murky, stagnant waters. This is where they will most likely pick up parasites and other diseases, which can be passed along to your fish.

BRINE SHRIMP—The brine shrimp in your local pet shop are one of the best food sources

FIVE GREAT GOLDFISH FOODS

Live brine shrimp

Complete flake food

Freeze-dried tubifex worms

Water fleas

Frozen bloodworm

Dried foods can be prepared in a number of ways, including flakes, or compressed into pellets, also known as granules (which are bite-size chunks), or tablets.

available for fish of any type. And of all the live food available, these are the safest, because they do not carry diseases and are easy to care for. And goldfish love them!

EARTHWORMS—Earthworms are rich in protein and are an interesting dietary change for your goldfish. They are particularly valuable to

FIVE HOUSEHOLD SCRAPS THAT MAKE GREAT TREATS

A small piece of lettuce

Canned peas

Crumbled cheese

Oat flakes

Wheat germ

Goldfish enjoy eating earth-worms, which may be available in your own backyard.

70

hobbyists and prized by goldfish during or preceding breeding season. They are also easily obtained. You can either search for them after showers in lawns and around ponds and lakes, or you can cultivate them in your backyard. Earthworms should be thoroughly cleaned with clear water before feeding to remove any pesticides that may endanger your goldfish.

If you have small goldfish, less than 4 inches long, you really should dice the earthworms up. If you have goldfish that are between 4 and 6 inches long, cut the worms into halves or thirds. Any goldfish over 6 inches long will be more than happy to swallow worms whole.

TUBIFEX—These long, thin, red worms, also known as sludgeworms, are not very pretty, but can be bought at the local pet store, where their chance of carrying disease is low. Like all live food, they are an excellent food source and will be gratefully appreciated by your fish.

Before feeding them to your fish, you must rinse them thoroughly in gently running water for at least one hour; if you can, do it for two more hours. Tubifex require a lot of work and are considered so risky that it is advised that you feed them to your goldfish only once or twice a month. While it is possible to breed these in a culture at your home, it's very difficult and is probably not worth the risk.

WHITEWORMS—Also known as microworms, these worms are white or beige. They can be bought in small single-serving amounts from your local pet shop. But they are also available in cultures. These cultures only last for approximately six weeks. If you suspect that the culture has gone bad, it is important that you dispose of the entire batch and keep none of the worms.

DAPHNIA—Also known as water flea larvae, these are an excellent food for your goldfish. However, goldfish should be fed this type of food in moderation, since too much of this type of food may act as a laxative and cause serious digestive problems in your fish. Moderation is the key when feeding any type of live food. Daphnia are easily obtained from your local pet shop in small quantities, or it is also possible to culture them at home.

DROSOPHILA—These are the larvae of *Drosophila*, the wingless (actually, vestigial-winged) fruit fly, so they won't try to fly away on you. They provide your fish with a tasty treat and an excellent food source. You can sometimes buy them at the local pet store, or you can culture them at home.

BLOODWORMS—Also known as two-winged fly larvae, these are usually in good supply year-round and can be purchased at your local pet

store. They are very difficult to cultivate at home. Because they are difficult to culture, they are usually commercially bred and therefore offer less risk of spreading disease to the hobbyist's fish. Again, these can be bought in small quantities for single or double servings.

FROZEN OR FREEZE-DRIED FOODS

Frozen or freeze-dried foods offer the best of the live world without any of the hassles of growing a culture. They also offer the protection of being disease-free. Freeze-dried and frozen foods include brine shrimp, krill (shrimp a little larger than brine), tubifex worms,

If you want healthy, active goldfish, you must vary their diets.

HOUSEHOLD FOODS
FOR YOUR FISH

Frozen (serve thawed): clams, mussels, shrimp, fish, lobster, crabmeat

Canned: the same as frozen, plus beans and peas

Raw: the same as frozen, plus spinach and lettuce

Cooked (baked, steamed, boiled): potato, beans, peas, egg yolk, broccoli, cauliflower, breadcrumbs

While live foods and foods other than flakes are highly desirable, it is important to know that no one group supplies everything your goldfish needs. Always selecting food from one group or another will lead to overload. Too many live foods and your goldfish may not have enough fats or carbohydrates in their diet. Too much of any one food may cause digestive problems too difficult to remedy.

mosquito larvae, daphnia and bloodworms. These are a great convenience to the hobbyist who wants to provide variety to his or her fish without having to deal with too much mess.

TABLE OR HOUSEHOLD FOODS

Table or household foods offer nutritional value and great variety to the goldfish diet. You can offer your goldfish fresh, frozen or canned clams, mussels, crabmeat, lobster or bits of raw fish. Baked or boiled beans, steamed cauliflower or broccoli and boiled or baked potato are all excellent additions as well. Fresh lettuce or spinach is also good. Raw bits of ground beef are especially prized.

These have to be given in moderation, and need to be diced or shredded so that they will be edible for your fish. Don't just throw a shrimp in—it will either sink to the bottom or float, or one of your fish will probably end up choking on it.

Don't offer your fish your table scraps unless they conform to what is listed. Also, no spices. Table food needs to be plain and chopped up. Also, any condiments that you put on your food will be floating around the aquarium and could possibly poison or injure your fish.

HOW TO FEED
YOUR FISH

The biggest problem when feeding goldfish is that they will eat to the point of bursting. They are gluttons—and that's the nicest thing that can be said about their table

Goldfish will eat as much and as often as they are fed, so it is important to control their food intake.

manners. Their food intake must be controlled. It is best to feed goldfish about as much as they can eat in a five-minute time period. It's best to do this two or three times a day—morning, afternoon, night—and always in the same spot.

To begin, put some flake food on the water and let them eat. If they finish all or most of it before the five minutes is up, add a little more until you feel that they have had enough. It's the same thing with live, freeze-dried or table food. It's that easy.

If you go away for a weekend, train a friend or family member to feed them while you are away.

Rules for Feeding Goldfish

1. Only feed them what they can eat in five minutes' time.

2. Feed them at the same time every day, once in the morning, once in the afternoon, and once at night.

3. Always feed them at the same spot in the tank.

4. Don't overfeed the fish, no matter how humane you think you are being. More goldfish die, especially older ones, from overeating than from anything else.

CHAPTER EIGHT

To Good Health

Goldfish (like other tropicals) are subject to all kinds of diseases. Many are introduced with the addition of new fish. Many diseases are highly contagious; others are not. Though you may think you did everything you possibly could to protect your fish, even experts fall victim to these problems.

GOLDFISH AND DISEASES

One of the best ways to cure any fish is to separate it from the rest of the fish as quickly as possible. It should be placed in something called a "hospital tank." This should be set up, with carbon-less filters (a sponge filtration system is recommended), an air pump and stone, a heater, dim lighting and no gravel should be present. A small artificial

plant will help to keep your afflicted fish calm. The tank generally does not have to be very big. Depending on the size of your fish, a 10-gallon tank is usually fine.

Anytime you think you might have a diseased fish, it's always better to separate it, at least until you can determine whether its affliction is transmittable or not. Also, diseased or weak fish will often get picked on by healthier fish. Goldfish are no exception, and their bedside manner can be less than sympathetic. And, obviously, it's easier to medicate the fish properly when it's by itself.

All of the problems listed below, while some may not be contagious, will require treatment, sometimes something as simple as a change of diet. However, when you are attempting to feed your goldfish medicated food, it is important that the fish that is sick eats it. The idea is not to overmedicate the healthy fish. This is another reason to separate out sick fish.

Healthy goldfish rarely get sick. So when your fish get sick, it usually means that they have been weakened by poor water conditions, rapid temperature changes, bad lighting,

It is important to maintain your aquarium conditions properly so that your fish's environment remains as disease-free as possible.

75

bad food or any number of other things.

COMMERCIAL REMEDIES

Commercial remedies, which are also known as proprietary medications (in liquid or tablet form), are excellent for beginners. If possible, discuss the problem with someone at your local pet store and let that person advise you on the best commercial remedies the store carries. Follow the directions exactly. Especially with fancy goldfish, caution must be maintained.

WHAT'S WRONG WITH MY FISH?

Listed below are some diseases, infestations and pests that afflict goldfish. If any of the following symptoms appear you will need to begin treatment immediately. If you cannot diagnose the problem, speak with your local fish dealer or another hobbyist.

DISEASE	SYMPTOMS
ANCHOR WORM	A white worm protrudes from a red, agitated area on the fish's body. Infested fish rubs against anything it can in attempting to scrape off the parasite (highly contagious). Cause: Lernaea crustacean Treatment: Remove parasite with tweezers, treat wound with mercurochrome.
BODY SLIME DISEASE	The protective slime coating grows white and starts peeling off, as if the fish were shedding or molting. The fins are eventually covered as well (highly contagious). Cause: Costia, trichodina, chilodonella or cyclochaeta parasites Treatment: Malachite green formula, and frequent water changes
CONSTIPATION, INDIGESTION	Fish very inactive, usually rests at the bottom of the tank. More likely than not, its abdomen swells or bulges (not contagious). Cause: Overfeeding, incorrect nutrition Treatment: Add one teaspoon magnesium sulfate for each two gallons. Fast your fish for three days, and then feed a varied diet including live foods.
DROPSY (KIDNEY BLOAT)	The belly bloats noticeably and the scales stick out like a pinecone (may be contagious). Cause: Organ failure from old age or poor water conditions Treatment: Antibacterial given though medicated foods. Improve the water conditions.

DISEASE	SYMPTOMS
FIN OR TAIL ROT	Fins have missing parts; eventually become shredded. Entire fin will be eaten away (contagious). Cause: Bacterial infection Treatment: Use proprietary medication. Add one tablespoon of aquarium salt for each five gallons of water in the hospital tank to help with osmoregulation.
FISH LICE	Round, disk-shaped creatures that clamp onto host and refuse to let go. Infected fish will rub up against objects in the tank in an effort to scrape these pests off (highly contagious). Cause: Argulus parasite Treatment: Remove parasite with tweezers. Apply an antiseptic solution to the wound.
FUNGUS	Fuzzy growth, different from velvet because it is more whitish and easier to notice (highly contagious). Cause: Saprolegnia fungus Treatment: Proprietary fungus medication. In advanced cases, the fungus can be blotted off of the body with a cotton swab dipped in mercurachrome.
GILL FLUKE	Gills swell up pink and red and the fish spend lots of time near the surface trying to suck in air. Pus-like fluid will be exuded from the gills at this time (contagious). Cause: Dactylogyrus fluke Treatment: Proprietary fluke medication in hospital tank, emergency cleaning on main tank
HYDRA	Fry die and are half-eaten or dissolved. Check for cannibalism first among fry (not contagious). Cause: Hydra Treatment: Complete water change

WHAT'S WRONG WITH MY FISH?

DISEASE	SYMPTOMS
ICH	Raised white spots about the size of a salt or sugar granule appear on the body and fins (highly contagious). Cause: Ichthyopthirius parasite Treatment: Proprietary ich remedy (malachite green or formalin), Frequent water changes in main tank, which must be medicated as well.
MOUTH FUNGUS	White cottony growth on mouth. Sometimes this spreads toward the gills (contagious). Cause: Columnaris bacteria Treatment: Proprietary mouth fungus treatment with antibiotic follow up
POP EYE	Fish's eyes begin to protrude in a very abnormal way (not contagious). Cause: Usually poor water conditions Treatment: Improve water conditions.
SKIN FLUKE	Swelled-up coat of some sort. Host fish is constantly trying to rub itself against object to scrape off the infection (contagious). Cause: Gyrodactylus parasite Treatment: Proprietary skin fluke treatment, Formalin baths will help as well.

OLD-FASHIONED SALT BATH

This is the most time-tested cure-all of the fish world. Sometimes called progressive salt-water treatment, it is what the hospital tank most often stands for. It is very simple and has been known to cure ich, fungus, velvet, tail rot and other malignancies. Many experts swear by it.

Place the fish in the hospital tank and add one teaspoon of table salt (not iodized) for each gallon of water. Add the same amount of salt that night and twice

78

DISEASE	SYMPTOMS
SWIM BLADDER	Fish swim on their sides, upside down or will somersault as they attempt to swim. Sometimes they can be found either at the bottom or at the top of the tank (not contagious). Cause: Physical injury or bacterial infection Treatment: Treat with antibiotic in a shallow tank. Do frequent water changes.
TUMORS	Obvious lumps, bumps, protrusions, sometimes they look like a large blister or wart (usually not contagious). Cause: Cancer Treatment: None known. Destroy the fish if it begins to suffer.
ULCERS	Large red ulcers, boils, dark reddening and bleeding (highly contagious). Cause: Bacterial Treatment: Antibiotics
VELVET	Fuzzy area grows with a yellow or golden color (highly contagious). Cause: Piscinoodinium parasite Treatment: Proprietary malachite green formula

79

the next day, again in the morning and at night. If there is no improvement by the third or fourth day, add one more teaspoon (just one) of salt each day. On the ninth and tenth days, make progressive water changes and check for results.

EMERGENCY CLEANING

This is the most severe treatment any tank can get and should only be used as a last resort. If any of the infestations mentioned below strike an entire tank, you need to make an

You should always isolate your infected fish until the disease or infestation is cured.

emergency cleaning. Place all the fish in the hospital tank and begin treatment. Then turn your attention to the aquarium.

The aquarium must be thoroughly cleaned and totally restarted. Throw out the filter medium and save as little as possible.

Empty out the contents of the tank. Rinse the walls of the tank, the gravel, and the filter with hot water. Make sure to rinse extra-thoroughly. Do the same to any plastic plants and rocks If you had any live plants, throw them out— don't use them for any other purpose. Replace the filter medium and the airstones, etc. If you have a heater, wash it with hot water and rinse it thoroughly.

CHAPTER NINE

Breeding Goldfish

One of the best ways that any aquarium keeper can improve his or her knowledge is through breeding. Hobbyists who breed their fish can obtain more detailed accounts of their pet's social habits, feeding patterns and physical needs. One of the most important reasons why aquarium hobbyists should breed fish is so they can help keep our earth's aquatic species alive for future generations of fishkeepers to enjoy.

Don't let anyone tell you that there is only one method of breeding goldfish. Each breeder has his own little tricks and tips that work well for him. But, there are always better methods of breeding that are still waiting to be discovered. Always be willing to exchange information with other breeders. Only through communication can we ever hope to become successful at any aquatic endeavor.

KEEP A RECORD

One of the most important aspects of breeding any type of aquarium fish is keeping a good written record of your activities. A small notebook or log book will work well to record important breeding information such as age, sex, temperament, color, number of eggs or fry, social behavior, size and health history. If you have a computer, you can always transfer the data to a disk, so you can modify it as needed. Taking photos of your fish during spawning time will also provide you with a good permanent record.

OBTAINING BREEDING STOCK

The first thing you want to do when breeding your goldfish is to look for good stock. You can obtain goldfish through your local pet center and on the Internet. If you have friends who enjoy keeping goldfish as much as you do, you might be able to trade pairs with them.

When choosing goldfish for breeding purposes, there are several physical attributes that you should keep an eye out for, such as a good

body shape, erect fins, proper head-growth for the species, and a good social disposition. If you begin with several physically healthy specimens, you will have a greater chance of producing vigorous young through a strong genetic code. Never attempt to breed unhealthy goldfish, especially if they have just been cured of disease. Many diseases can lead to damage of the eggs through improper nutrition during the illness. Always begin breeding with the healthiest fish that you can find. The following list will give you a good idea of what to look for.

- The goldfish should not have ulcers, sores or skin problems such as missing scales or blemishes.

- The goldfish's stomach should be well-rounded, of normal proportion, and not sunken or concave.

- The goldfish should have flowing or erect fins that are not ragged, torn or missing.

- The goldfish's body color should be rich and not faded.

- The goldfish's eyes should be clear, alert and not cloudy.

- The goldfish's waste should be dark in color and not pale.

- The goldfish's fins should not be collapsed or tightly clamped shut.

- The goldfish should not have any visible parasites such as ich or velvet.

- The goldfish's scales should be flat and smooth, and not protruding away from its body.

- The goldfish should swim with ease and not continually fight to maintain its normal position in the water.

- The goldfish should be breathing normally, not gulping for air near the filter or the top of the tank.

- The goldfish should not be lurking in the corners of the aquarium or hiding behind the decorations.

THE BREEDING TANK

A 10- or 20-gallon aquarium will work great for a breeding tank. Small tanks will allow you to keep track of your breeding pairs and their eggs. The aquarium should be placed in an area that does not have a lot of human traffic. The tank should be thoroughly rinsed with clean water before you use it for breeding. A tight-fitting hood will

Breeding helps fishkeeping hobbyists better understand the nature of their pets.

Always begin breeding with the healthiest fish that you can find.

help to prevent chemicals and dirt from entering the breeding water. Research has suggested that intense lighting can damage eggs. Keep the lighting in your breeding tank as low as possible. Substrate is optional.

Filtration

Filters will supply oxygen and will also keep wastes that can destroy eggs from building up. A sponge filter will create current, but will not cause excess turbulence that is often produced by larger power filters. A sponge filter provides simple biological filtration without excessive turbulence, which can injure eggs.

Plants

A few live or artificial plants will help to provide security and make your spawners feel like they are in a natural setting. Live plants should be thoroughly cleaned before they are added to the spawning tank, because they often carry snails and small worms that can harm eggs and newly hatched fry.

Water Conditions

The water in your spawning tank must be the same as the water from which your pairs were taken. Eggs and young fry can easily be damaged by fluctuations in pH, so it is important to monitor it carefully during spawning and rearing. Young fry and eggs will have problems resulting from the presence of too much waste in the water. Poor water conditions can destroy eggs, so make sure that you do not overfeed. If possible, carefully change a little bit of the water each day in the spawning and growout tanks.

CONDITIONING YOUR BREEDERS

When seasonal rainstorms sweep over a fish's natural environment, large supplies of live insects are often deposited on the water's surface. This new abundance of live food usually signals the beginning of the spring or early summer spawning cycle. Live foods such as brine shrimp help to condition your goldfish for spawning. In the spawning tank, you can help to duplicate a natural rainstorm and improve conditioning through frequent water

changes with clean de-mineralized water. An increase in barometric pressure will often make aquarium fish breed more actively right before or during a rainstorm.

A change in temperature can stimulate spawning. Dropping the temperature a few degrees overnight and then slowly raising it back up in the morning can help to condition your goldfish. During this temperature change, live foods should be fed frequently.

WHY SOME WILL NOT SPAWN

There are several reasons why a particular pair of fish may not spawn. The fish may be too young, too old, in bad health, of the same sex, one may be sterile or the aquarium conditions may not be right. If your goldfish do not spawn right away, don't quit. Everything takes time. Try a new method, and begin again until you find the right conditions for your particular species.

COURTSHIP AND SPAWNING

Courtship among goldfish often consists of the male shoving the

female against plants while he shimmies from side to side. During spawning, the goldfish's eggs and sperm are spewed into the water, and often stick to plants and decorations. After a few minutes have passed, the fish will separate for a short time and then repeat the spawning ritual over and over for a period of several hours.

THE EGGS

Goldfish eggs will usually look like small white or transparent spheres. Many females can lay thousands of eggs at one time. The eggs will usually be incubated in five to seven days, depending on the temperature of the breeding tank's water. If the parents begin to eat the eggs, they should be removed at once. Eggs are susceptible to fungus, and should be watched carefully. When an egg develops fungus, it will turn dark white and then start to look fuzzy. You can add a little methylene blue to the water to help inhibit the spread of this damaging disease.

GROWTH

After about three or four days, eye spots, body color and a beating heart can be seen in the developing embryos. Near the seventh day, they will hatch.

FEEDING FRY

Young fry should be fed three times a day. Baby brine shrimp, crushed yolk from hard-boiled eggs and liquid fry foods will all help them to achieve maximum growth. Make sure that you skim uneaten food off of the water surface after each feeding. Frequent water changes will also be required to keep environmental conditions at their best.

CHAPTER TEN

Resources

BOOKS

Andrew, Dr. Chris. *Fancy Goldfishes.* Morris Plains, NJ: Tetra Press, 1987.

Barrie, Anmarie. *Goldfish as a New Pet.* Neptune, NJ: TFH Publications, 1990.

Coborn, John. *Howell Beginner's Guide to Goldfish.* New York: Howell Book House, 1985.

DeVito, Carlo. *The Goldfish: An Owner's Guide to a Happy Healthy Pet.* New York, NY: Howell Book House, 1996.

Goldfish Society of America. *The Official Guide to Goldfish.* Neptune, NJ: TFH Publications, 1991.

Paradise, Paul. *Goldfish.* Neptune, NJ: TFH Publications, 1992.

Piers, Helen. *Taking Care of Your Goldfish.* Hauppauge, NY: Barron's, 1993.

Wardley Coporation. *Fin Facts Aquarium Handbook.* Secaucus, NJ: Wardley Corporation, 1992.

There are several places that you can find aquarium keeping information, such as library books, magazines, fish clubs and on the Internet.

MAGAZINES

In order to keep up with rapidly changing equipment, organizations, health and breeding technology, beginning hobbyists can read aquarium magazines to learn more about current information. Magazines are usually printed on a monthly basis, have beautiful pictures and carry informative, up-to-date aquarium tips.

AQUARIUM FISH
P.O Box 6040
Mission Viejo, CA 92690
(949) 855-8822

FRESHWATER AND MARINE AQUARIUM
PO Box 487
Sierra Madre, CA 91024
(818) 355-1476

PRACTICAL FISHKEEPING
c/o Motorsport
RR1 Box 200 D
Jonesburg, MO 63351
(314) 488-3113

TROPICAL FISH HOBBYIST
One Neptune Plaza
Neptune City, NJ 07753
(732) 988-8400

MORE INFORMATION ABOUT GOLDFISH

Other Useful Resources – Web Sites and Internet Links

There are many Web sites that can provide you with goldfish information and help you learn more about your new pet. The following Web sites are loaded with helpful information, purchasing sites and provide several other useful goldfish links.

http://www.goldfishconnection.com/ – The Goldfish Connection

http://www.chinainfornet.com/comps/goldfish/index.htm – Grace Goldfish Farm

http://www.finnsaquatics.com/ – Finns Aquatics

http://www.bestfish.com/index.html – Aquatics Unlimited

http://www.fishlinkcentral.com/ – Fish Link Central

http://www.mops.on.ca/ – Mail Order Pet Supplies

Clubs and Organizations

Fish clubs and organizations are a great way to learn more about goldfish care and communicate with other hobbyists who share your interests in fishkeeping.

AMERICAN AQUARIST SOCIETY, INC.
Box 100
3901 Hatch Blvd.
Sheffield, AL 35660

CANADIAN ASSOCIATION OF AQUARIUM CLUBS
95 East 31st Street
Hamilton, Ontario, Canada L8V 3N9

GOLDFISH SOCIETY OF AMERICA
9107 West 154 Street
Prior Lake, MN 55372-2119

GOLDFISH SOCIETY OF GREAT BRITAIN
Ms. Christine Griffin
23 Green Lane
Northgate, Crawley
West Sussex RH10 2JX, England

INTERNATIONAL AQUARIUM SOCIETY (IAS)
PO Box 373
Maine, NY 13802-0373

89

YOUR ESSENTIAL *Goldfish* INFORMATION SHEET

Tear me out!

Put a picture of your goldfish
in this box

Your Goldfish's Name

Your Goldfish's Breed ______________________

Identifying Features ______________________

Where Your Goldfish Came From ______________________

Date of Birth ______________________

Your Goldfish's Veterinarian ______________________

Address ______________________

Phone Number ______________________

Favorite Foods ______________________

Your Goals for Your Goldfish

Hobby

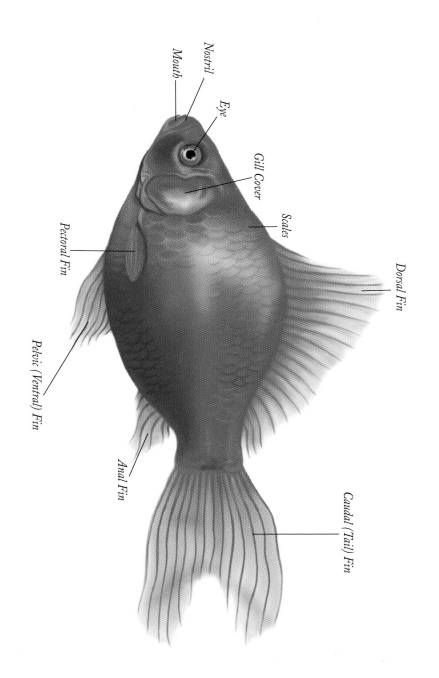

Mouth

Nostril

Eye

Gill Cover

Scales

Dorsal Fin

Pectoral Fin

Pelvic (Ventral) Fin

Anal Fin

Caudal (Tail) Fin